# WORDS *from the* WATER'S EDGE

MYSTICAL WRITINGS *of* LLEWELLYN VAUGHAN-LEE

# WORDS *from the* WATER'S EDGE

## MYSTICAL WRITINGS *of* LLEWELLYN VAUGHAN-LEE

The Golden Sufi Center®
Publishing

First published in the United States in 2025 by
The Golden Sufi Center
P.O. Box 456
Point Reyes, California 94956
www.goldensufi.org

First printing 2025.



Cover photo by Anat Vaughan-Lee.
Printed and bound in the USA.

ISBNs
*paperback:* 978-1941394-53-3
*pdf:* 978-1941394-54-0
*epub:* 978-1941394-55-7

Library of Congress Cataloging-in-Publication Data

Names: Vaughan-Lee, Llewellyn, author.
Title: Words from the water's edge : mystical writings of Llewellyn Vaughan-Lee / Llewellyn Vaughan-Lee.
Description: Point Reyes, California : The Golden Sufi Center, 2025. | Includes bibliographical references.
Identifiers: LCCN 2024052753 (print) | LCCN 2024052754 (ebook) | ISBN 9781941394533 (paperback) | ISBN 9781941394540 (pdf) | ISBN 9781941394557 (epub)
Subjects: LCSH: Mysticism. | Spiritual life. | Human ecology--Religious aspects.
Classification: LCC BL625 .V386 2025 (print) | LCC BL625 (ebook) | DDC 297.4--dc23/eng/20250113
LC record available at https://lccn.loc.gov/2024052753
LC ebook record available at https://lccn.loc.gov/2024052754

# CONTENTS

*To the Masters of Love, the friends of God,*
*who have helped guide humanity for millennia.*

# FOREWORD

Walking along the shoreline here in Northern California, feeling the waves breaking around my feet, I look out on the water, knowing that it stretches over many horizons. The ocean here can be dangerous, with sudden sneaker waves, riptides, seas turning rough. One treads carefully on the water's edge, respecting this wildness, knowing this ocean is never really safe. And yet at the same time this edge of vastness is so familiar, echoing the inner worlds in which I have lived, the vast empty horizons behind my eyes.

And from this place that is no place I would like to share a collection of sayings, of words, phrases written since the time I started teaching. These are words that sing to me, that speak of this soul's journey of no end which I have been travelling since I was sixteen, and especially since I sat at my teacher's feet when I was nineteen. They speak of the mystery, the wonder, the pain, the tears, and the endless love that have taken me. They are a taste of this journey that, especially in later years, has been woven together with the Earth's journey in these troubled, broken times. Because there came a time when the sorrow of my own soul and that of the Earth were bonded together, and my love was not just for an inner Beloved, but also for this beautiful, suffering being we call our Home.

These sayings leave traces of a lifetime walking between the worlds, holding a thread that has taken me into the beyond of the beyond, as well as back to the simple bliss of my garden, the red-tailed hawk sitting on a branch outside my window. And the ocean remains just over the hill, as wild and endless as the empty spaces in the heart, and the silence that has always called to me.

# 1

# LOVER AND BELOVED

*In the whole of the Universe there is nothing else*
*but the Lover and the Beloved.*

Irina Tweedie

Sufis all sing the one song, that of lover and Beloved. The Beloved looks into the heart of the lover and ignites it with the spark of remembrance, with the call for the journey. This spark becomes a fire that burns us, that empties us of everything except love. Through the fire of love we come to know the essence of love, the greatest secret hidden within every cell of creation. Finding what we really are, we become lost in the mystical truth of humanity, that there is nothing other than God.

LOVE IS A FIRE: THE SUFI'S
MYSTICAL JOURNEY HOME

The mystical relationship of lover and Beloved is one of mankind's greatest secrets. It embraces all of creation and yet takes place within the human heart. The soul's love affair with God is a passion that transforms the whole human being and reveals the hidden face of the world. The mystical journey is an unfolding of this love affair, a giving of oneself to God through love. Because this love belongs to oneness, it takes us back to oneness. The wayfarer is brought home from a life of separation to an experience of being merged into God.

THE SIGNS OF GOD

The Sufis have been known as the people of the secret because they carry this secret of love, the oneness of lover and Beloved.

LOVE IS A FIRE: THE SUFI'S
MYSTICAL JOURNEY HOME

It is the Beloved who is seeking us, calling to us, longing for us. We always think that we are the seeker, but the deeper mystery is that we are the called.

Catching the Thread: Sufism, Dreamwork, and Jungian Psychology

Spiritual life is a response to a call. Of our own accord we would never turn away from the world and begin the long and painful journey home. But Someone calls to us, calls to us from within the depths of our heart, awakening our own deepest longing. This call is like a golden thread that we follow, guiding us deeper and deeper within, always pointing to the beyond. It is both intimate and elusive, for it does not belong to the mind, but to the deepest core of our being. We hear it most easily when the conscious mind is still, which can be in meditation or when we are surrounded by the beauty of nature.

Catching the Thread: Sufism, Dreamwork, and Jungian Psychology

The Sufi relates to God not as a judge, nor as a father figure, nor as the creator, but as our own Beloved, who is so close, so near, so tender.

Love is a Fire: The Sufi's Mystical Journey Home

The secret of the mystical journey is that in the core of every human heart is a connection of love that directly links lover and Beloved.

"LIVING THE MOMENT OF THE SOUL"

It is here, in the secret recesses of the heart, that the relationship with the Beloved takes place. The Beloved was always here, waiting to be born into consciousness. But we need to prepare ourself for this meeting, we need to align ourself to the inner vibrations of the Self. How can you notice your invisible lover when your consciousness is filled with the outer world? How can you enter the sacred space of your own heart wearing boots muddied with the desires of the ego? Here lies the esoteric meaning of the immaculate conception. For the Beloved to be conceived as a living presence we need to go through a process of inner purification.

THE BOND WITH THE BELOVED: THE MYSTICAL RELATIONSHIP OF LOVER AND BELOVED

The journey of the lover is a one-way street of love, and our tears carry us into an abyss of longing, of aloneness and anguish. But in this desert of desolation when despair seems our only company, something is born, something infinitely precious and tender beyond our understanding. Our soul senses the intimacy of its Beloved, who is as close as "the tears that run between the eye and the eye-lid." We begin to experience a love affair that is as intoxicating as it is painful, as wondrous as it is terrifying. We are awakened to the softness of the Beloved's touch, to the sweetness of love's embrace.

THE SIGNS OF GOD

In the states of nearness the lover experiences an intimacy with the Beloved which carries the softness and ecstasy of love.

LOVE IS A FIRE: THE SUFI'S MYSTICAL JOURNEY HOME

When love reveals its real nature we come to know that there is neither lover nor Beloved. There is no one to pray and no one to pray to. We do not even know that we are lost; we return from these states of merging only knowing that we gave ourself and were taken. Our gift of ourself was accepted so completely that we knew nothing. We looked towards our Beloved who took us in love's arms, embraced us in oneness, dissolved us in nearness. For so many years we cried out, we called to our Beloved, and when love came the meeting was so intimate that we knew nothing.

THE CIRCLE OF LOVE

There is a Sufi teaching that it is through the heart of the lover that the Beloved is able to see and know Itself, to witness the One within creation. The more polished the heart of the lover, the clearer this divine perception, until, in Ibn 'Arabi's words, "the mystic is the pupil in the eye of humanity," the place where divine revelation is witnessed. This is the secret hidden within the human being, that "man is My secret and I am his secret."[1] But it is not just the oneness of the Divine that is waiting to be experienced through the mystic heart, but the very secret of creation: that in all the forms of existence the hidden nature of the formless is revealed.

INTO THE LIGHT AND BACK AGAIN:
A MYSTIC'S JOURNEY

In the West we are so addicted to the notion of progress that we project this idea onto our spiritual life, and can become very confused by the dawning realization that the Beloved whom we seek is always with us, that we are always close but do not know it. The spiritual path is a process of revealing the nearness, the intimacy of love that is always with us.

THE CIRCLE OF LOVE

In our busy lives it is so easy to forget the Divine, to be immersed in our own problems and our own selves. The mystic knows that what really matters is the inner connection of the heart in which our heart opens and cries. It is something so simple and yet so easily overlooked.

PRAYER OF THE HEART IN CHRISTIAN AND SUFI MYSTICISM

The bond between the lover and the Beloved is the strongest link with the beyond, and it is through this link that grace can flow into the world.

THE BOND WITH THE BELOVED: THE MYSTICAL RELATIONSHIP OF LOVER AND BELOVED

The Beloved speaks most directly to us through the language of love because this is the simplest connection, the most direct expression of the Divine. Love is the truth underneath all of life's manifestations, the primal note in the symphony of creation. The work of the mystic is to hold this note for humanity. Within it lies the secret of our Beloved's relationship to us and to all of life.

SPIRITUAL POWER: HOW IT WORKS

In the whole of the universe there is only one love story, that of lover and Beloved. And yet this one story is lived in millions of ways, each story a unique fragrance of love. Every cell in creation lives its own love story, its longing for the Source. Human beings have the capacity to make this story conscious, to know the nature of their hidden loving.

FRAGMENTS OF A LOVE STORY: REFLECTIONS ON THE LIFE OF A MYSTIC

# 2

# THE POWER OF LOVE

*Love is the Greatest Power in Creation.*

Love is everywhere, like summer sunlight, like green grass in Spring. It is the wind rustling the leaves, the water flowing in the stream. Love is a presence, not something that comes and goes. And this love holds me; it is a substance that sustains me. Without it I would be entirely lost, a traveler between the worlds with nowhere to go.

Into the Light and Back Again:
A Mystic's Journey

On this journey love is the power that will take us Home. Love is the most powerful force in the universe and it resides within the heart of each of us. But this love needs to be awakened. The heart needs to be activated so that it can come to know its primordial passion, this link of love that runs through the world and is our own essence.

Love is a Fire: The Sufi's
Mystical Journey Home

Love is the dominant force, and in its light there is no deception.

Awakening the World: A Global
Dimension to Spiritual Practice

Love is life's greatest gift. We seek for love, and yet it is all around and within us. It belongs to the oneness of life, to every dewdrop on every leaf, to the spider spinning its web, the child looking at the stars. If we open our senses and open our hearts, we can feel its presence. Love is life speaking to us of its real mystery. And in that conversation so many things can happen, so many miracles can be born, the small unsuspecting miracles that we often do not notice—like momentary sunlight from behind a cloud, a flower where a seed unexpectedly sprouted, a smile from a stranger. Despite all of its distortions, pain, and suffering, this world belongs to love, just as each of us belongs to love. And just to know that we are part of this love is enough.

"Love: Life's Greatest Gift"

Once you have tasted the ocean of love's oneness it is in your blood. It is always calling you, sometimes from afar and sometimes so close you can feel its presence. It is like a lover you always long for.

Fragments of a Love Story: Reflections on the Life of a Mystic

The journey continues, the journey always continues. And since the very beginning there have been souls, men and women of all races, called on this journey, drawn by love back to love, called to rediscover the essential oneness of lover and Beloved, the union of divine love. They have been called by many different names in different places and times, they are servants of God, lovers of God, mystics, fools of divine love. But these are just words for a mystery that takes place first deep within the heart, and then spreads to every cell of the body, to our thoughts and feelings, to our dreams, to the way we place our feet on the ground.

"A Return to Love: A Few Simple Words for Mystics and Lovers"

Longing takes us back to God, takes the lover back into the arms of the Beloved. This is the ancient path of the mystic, of those who are destined to make the journey to the further shores of love. Why we are called to this quest is always a mystery, for the ways of the heart cannot be understood by the mind. Love always draws us back to love, and longing is the fire that purifies us. Sufis know the secrets of love, of the way love takes and transforms us. They are the people of love who have kept alive the mysteries of divine loving, of what is hidden within the depths of the human being.

Love is a Fire: The Sufi's Mystical Journey Home

The great mystery is then not that this love is always present, but that it appears hidden from us, that we have forgotten how we are made of love. That we are love seeking love. And life's greatest gift is love waiting to be lived.

"Love: Life's Greatest Gift"

I first thought of the spiritual journey as a linear path towards a distant goal. Gradually, I came to realize that the spiritual journey is a closed circle of love in which we slowly come closer to the center of ourself, which is always present. In this journey there is no "progress" but a shifting of consciousness that unveils our own essential nature, "the face we had before we were born." As this spiral path unfolds, so our concepts of both ourself and the journey change, and we come to realize the deeper truth: that the traveler, the journey, and the goal are all one.

The Face Before I Was Born:
A Spiritual Autobiography

The pain of love makes us inwardly abandon everything we hold precious, our attachments, even our beliefs. We become so thirsty for just another sip that we sell or give away everything—nothing else matters. Even our self-respect, our self-worth—all is destroyed, dissolved, melted by love and longing.

Love is a Fire: The Sufi's
Mystical Journey Home

For the Sufi the death of the ego takes place in the arena of love. Entering this arena, we turn our back on the values of the world and our instincts of self-preservation. Love is the energy that breaks down our patterns of resistance and transforms us. Love is the energy of oneness in which lover and Beloved are united since before the beginning of time. Deep within the heart there is a place that has no knowledge of duality or separation. The Sufis call this innermost chamber of the heart the "heart of hearts." The heart of hearts is the locus of the spiritual quest, the arena of transformation.

THE PARADOXES OF LOVE

The relationship between teacher and disciple is one of the great esoteric secrets of humanity. It is a bond within the heart that takes us from the world of the ego and the mind to the further shores of love. It is made out of the purest substance that exists in this world, the secret substance of divine love.

FRAGMENTS OF A LOVE STORY: REFLECTIONS ON THE LIFE OF A MYSTIC

Love calls to us in many different ways. Yet while most people seek for love in the tangle of human relationships, the mystic is drawn deeper under the surface—in Rumi's words, "return to the root of the root of your own being." And here we begin to discover one of life's greatest secrets: how love is at the Source of all that exists, *is* the Source of all that exists. Love is not just a feeling between people, but a substance, an energy, a divine spark that is present within everything. And it is this deepest essence—this substance of love—that we need to nourish us.

"LOVE: LIFE'S GREATEST GIFT"

Those who wish to enter this path must accept that they can never explain either to themselves or to others the mysterious inner unfolding that is taking them home.

CATCHING THE THREAD: SUFISM, DREAMWORK, AND JUNGIAN PSYCHOLOGY

Spiritual life is a state of being, a natural state of being with oneself and with God. Because it is a state of being we can never find it, but through our searching we tear away the veils that separate us from this consciousness of the heart. What we discover is that we know how to be with God. A familiarity and awe, an intimacy and distance are woven into the substance of the soul. Each of us will experience and express this state of being in our own way, for "Each instinctively knows their manner of prayer and glorification." (Sura 24:41)

IN THE COMPANY OF FRIENDS: DREAMWORK WITHIN A SUFI GROUP

The mystical path is the most difficult, demanding, dangerous, and intoxicating journey one can ever make. It takes one into the depths of the heart, into the abyss and endless love one finds there. It leads you from the known into the unknown, and then further, into the unknowable, into a darkness brighter than any light. Nothing can prepare you for the heart's journey, for the places it can take you, the depths and heights that are within you. So many times you think you are crazy, bewildered and lost.

FRAGMENTS OF A LOVE STORY: REFLECTIONS ON THE LIFE OF A MYSTIC

Love speaks to our soul and to our body. Love includes all the senses—taste and touch, smell, sight, and sound. Love by its very nature includes everything. It can be found anywhere, because it is everywhere. The mystic uncovers the simple secret: that in truth love flows through everything—sweet, tender, aching, knowing, as well as dark and passionate. And as this primal energy, this greatest power, awakens within us, within our heart, our soul, always it draws us deeper into its own mystery, into the secret of oneness, what the Sufis call the unity of being.

"LOVER AND BELOVED: MYSTICAL LOVE IN SUFISM"

The price of love is our own self, which we pay with our tears and suffering. When you are going through it, you wonder how long you can last, how you can survive this endless longing, the bleeding, the pain, as the "I" is being torn apart by love. And then one day you notice that the pain has gone, instead there is an intimacy, a secret meeting, a deep knowing that you are with your Beloved.

FRAGMENTS OF A LOVE STORY: REFLECTIONS ON THE LIFE OF A MYSTIC

Half a century ago I awoke to the call of wild geese, and this calling led me deep within the heart, into the rich textures of human experiences, as well as into other dimensions. And now I feel called by a skyline beyond the horizons of any journey. And yet still I remain here, with two feet on the ground, knowing nothing except the power of love and the presence of the unknown.

INTO THE LIGHT AND BACK AGAIN: A MYSTIC'S JOURNEY

The real nature of mystical prayer is to draw us into this most intimate mystery of divine love. The mystic comes to know that the essence of prayer is this hidden secret of the heart—that there is only oneness. For when the heart is open and looks towards God it is awakened to the revelation of divine unity. This state of prayer is a merging and melting that transcends the mind and its notions of duality: the heart overwhelms us with divine presence that obliterates any sense of our own self.

PRAYER OF THE HEART IN CHRISTIAN AND SUFI MYSTICISM

The experience of union with God is not the end of the journey, but the beginning of a new life in which the mystic becomes more and more deeply immersed in divine presence, more and more lost in God.

SUFISM: THE TRANSFORMATION OF THE HEART

But there is a need for something to be made known, for the secrets of the heart to be made public, for the music of the soul to be played....

For centuries lovers of God have held the secrets of divine love within their own hearts, shared only with initiates. But this knowledge needs to be made public, the song of Love's Oneness to be heard. If the music of divine love is not played in the marketplace, life will lose its meaning, and the collective despair of the soul will be too terrible to imagine.

THE SIGNS OF GOD

To search is to find what the heart has always known, that there are no boundaries to love.

FRAGMENTS OF A LOVE STORY: REFLECTIONS ON THE LIFE OF A MYSTIC

Love is present within our own heart, within every breath, within every cell of our bodies and the whole of creation.

"LOVE, LIFE'S GREATEST GIFT"

During these last difficult, exhausting years, what has sustained me most has been love. Not the love of my earlier years on the path, the love of aspiration and longing, passion, heartbreak, and bliss. I have been taken to a place of love, and I know that love is all around, like air to breath. Love is now easy, not something to be longed for or sought. In this love there do not seem to be two; it is no longer the drama of lover and Beloved. It just is.

INTO THE LIGHT AND BACK AGAIN: A MYSTIC'S JOURNEY

Love is the most powerful force in the universe. Love draws us back to love, love uncovers love, love makes us whole and love takes us Home. In the depths of the soul we are loved by God. This is the deepest secret of being human, the bond of love that is at the core of our being and belongs to all that exists.

"UNITY AND THE POWER OF LOVE"

The eternal moment is outside of time, is not a part of our past or our future, and yet it is lived amidst all our everyday activities. It is in the eternal moment that love is born. Love does not belong to time, and its timeless quality is well known to all lovers. The lover has to learn to still the mind in order to catch the moment and stay true to love's unfolding. Wayfarers tread a path that leads from illusions of time to the eternal moment that belongs to the soul.

THE SIGNS OF GOD

The nonexistence of the mystic is one of the secrets of the path. The mystical path takes us from being to nonbeing, a state of nonexistence that is dynamically alive and full of love. On the Sufi path this is the stage of *fana* that leads to *baqa*, abiding in God.

LIGHT OF ONENESS

Silence is singing with love. There is love that exists in forms, sounds, and activities—we feel its presence in beauty, are touched by its joy. But there is also love present in emptiness, in silence, in space—a love that does not require recognition, that just is. The mystic is absorbed by this love that at once takes her into the infinite and grounds her in the web of life, for silence is an open passageway between the worlds.

Through spiritual practices like meditation or watching the breath, mystics become familiar with this silence. It happens quite naturally that we dwell in silence, for silence pervades the depths into which the mystic dives again and again. This silence is undefined and speaks to us of the undefined vistas of our own being, and the greater mystery that pervades everything.

For Love of the Real: A Story of Life's Mystical Secret

The path of love takes the lover behind the veils of creation into the ocean of love's oneness where all semblance of self dissolves. In this infinite ocean where "swimming ends always in drowning," the lover merges into the infinite emptiness that is at the core of creation. Love's truth is a vortex of nothingness out of which is born the dance of life, the opposites that spiral into manifestation. From the formless emptiness the multiplicity of forms comes into being.

Love is a Fire: The Sufi's Mystical Journey Home

# 3

# LIGHT UPON LIGHT

*Light rises towards light*
*and light comes down upon light,*
*"and it is light upon light."*
*... this is the secret of the mystical approach.*

NAJM AL-DIN KUBRA

We have in us a divine spark that you can see. It's a light that shines in the human being. It's our direct access to Truth, our direct access to God. The purpose of most of the spiritual practices that exist are to awaken that spark to give it life, to give it energy, so that it can transform you. One of the energies that comes from this spark is love.

"We Are All One: Interview"

Our Higher Self carries a light that belongs to God. When we are born, we carry a spark of this light into our human incarnation; it illuminates the experiences of our early childhood, often showing us a world that is fully alive, full of magic and wonder. But slowly, as the adult world closes around us, the spark of our Higher Self gets covered over by the dust and debris of the world, of our conditioning, our desires, our concern with success and failure, our need to compete; it "fades into the common light of day."[2]

Alchemy of Light: Working with the Primal Energies of Life

Recently I was sitting in an airport lounge full of people waiting to board a flight. For a few moments my eyes were opened, and I saw how each person was full of divine presence, how there was nothing other than God, God's light, God's love, God's beauty. And in the same few moments I also saw that these people did not know it. In this experience I realized that the real mystery is not that we are all divine, are filled with divine substance, but that we do not know it. *We do not know that we are a part of God.* This experience filled me with wonder, the wonder that part of the mystery of creation is that we have been allowed to forget the Divine. It is God's will that in us the Divine is forgotten, just as it is God's will that we are allowed to remember.

THE CIRCLE OF LOVE

Present in the here and now, and yet hidden amidst life's daily demands, is a world of light and love, the pure light of the Divine. The relationship of this world of light, *light upon light*, to the physical world, to our everyday interactions, to life's joys and sorrows, is one of the greatest mysteries. We come from this light, the Source, and we return to this pure light, which is both our own true nature—the light at the end of the tunnel of near-death experiences—and also the Divine that is within and around all that exists. And yet our human experience is that we are separate from this light, caught in a world of struggles and suffering, injustice and inequality. Similarly, we search for love, we long to be loved, even as it is our own deepest nature.

A HANDBOOK FOR SURVIVALISTS: CARING FOR THE EARTH, A SERIES OF MEDITATIONS

Our souls are made of a quality of light, a light that belongs to God and carries a knowing of its Source. Through this light the soul sees its way, the path it follows, the destiny that needs to be lived. Without this light there could be no evolution, no meaning to life.

Spiritual Power: How It Works

This light that is the essence of our essence is what calls to us within the heart, "the love within your love." I have experienced a touch of this light in the depths of my own meditation, even journeyed into a world made only of light. Certainly I have longed to return to the sun of suns, be lost in it. And yet always I have been drawn back, called by a human story, as if the elements of this world needed to tell me their secret. The spiritual path made me a piece of dust at the feet of my teacher, and I am still that dust.

"Walking Between Worlds"

The divine consciousness conceived within the heart of the lover is the knowledge of God's oneness, of the Beloved's unending presence and limitless love.

The Paradoxes of Love

On the pavement a group of schoolchildren was walking past the driveway with their teacher. They were probably on an outing; maybe they had been to the park. I noticed these young children crossing the entrance and suddenly I saw them in a way I have never seen human beings before or since. They were so full of light I could hardly look, and on each child's chest where the heart is, a huge radiance like the sun was shining. Each little child had this dynamic, brilliant light, this radiant sun, in the center of their being. The experience of the light, its brilliance and energy, was beautiful and overwhelming....

Later I came to realize that what I saw is the true nature of human beings—we are dynamic, luminous creatures of light.

THE FACE BEFORE I WAS BORN:
A SPIRITUAL AUTOBIOGRAPHY

Nothing is as it appears. The mystic uses the image of peeling the skins of an onion to describe how we discover our true essence, and it is the same with life. Images are built upon images, revelation upon revelation. It is all an illusion and it is all the Beloved.

SPIRITUAL POWER: HOW IT WORKS

Through meditation and inner work we create an inner space that is unpolluted by the desires of the ego and the chatter of the mind. Going within the heart, we learn to listen to the voice of the Beloved, the guidance of the Self.

SUFISM: THE TRANSFORMATION OF THE HEART

It is because of our wounds, our pain and our sadness, that we turn from the outer world and trace the thread of our own darkness back to its source. It leads us through the barriers of pain to the place of our own healing. But in the very process of making this journey, the light of consciousness which we carry with us transforms our darkness. The individual who arrives at the Source is very different from the person who set out upon the quest. During the course of this journey we have to accept and integrate what we find within us—our pain and our anger and all the many forms our darkness has taken.... We will have to accept ourselves as we really are. This then will be the chalice into which the Divine Wine can be poured.

CATCHING THE THREAD: SUFISM, DREAMWORK AND JUNGIAN PSYCHOLOGY

Confrontation and acceptance of the shadow are the cornerstone of all inner work.... The rejected and unacknowledged parts of oneself need to be loved and brought out of the darkness.

SUFISM: THE TRANSFORMATION OF THE HEART.

Through the mystery of inner work, darkness is turned into light. The chaos and confusion of our unconscious gradually and miraculously reveal a higher center of consciousness which is none other than our innermost essence, "the face we had before we were born." This is the Self, the Divine Child, which was always present within us, but hidden beneath layers of ego and conditioning.

SOURCE UNKNOWN

Sufis describe the heart as a mirror which the wayfarer polishes and polishes with aspiration and inner work, until no imperfection remains. Then the mirror of the heart can reflect the true light of the Beloved.

TRAVELLING THE PATH OF LOVE:
SAYINGS OF SUFI MASTERS

Gradually the focus of our journey shifts from the inner work of "polishing the mirror of the heart" to the simplicity of living a daily life with a heart that belongs to God.

THE CIRCLE OF LOVE

I had an English upbringing in which I never knew about love.... The family I grew up in, love was never mentioned, and I don't think it was very present either. There was material security, but there wasn't love. I can't remember, looking back in my childhood, love ever being mentioned. I was sent off to boarding school at the age of seven and there wasn't any love. There was lots of football and cricket but no love.

It wasn't until I was, must have been 29, and I remember the afternoon I was lying down in meditation in my teacher's meditation room, and suddenly there were these butterfly wings on the edge of my heart ... then slowly this love was infused into my body, into my being, first through the heart, and then it went into every cell of my body, and it was pure love. There was nobody there. There was no person. It was just love. It was just this essential quality of love that went from my heart through all of me, through the veins of my body, of my being, and I actually felt it in every cell of my body. This energy of love, that is so incredibly tender and powerful.

In meditation you can go beyond this outer world of forms, of images, and you can go deeper and deeper into what the Sufis call nonbeing, the nothingness, the dazzling darkness behind creation. And what I discovered is that there is a place where, out of the nothingness, out of the emptiness, love comes into existence. There is like a doorway, or like a stream coming out of the ground, out of this primal emptiness that is behind creation, out of this vast unknown, unknowable there is a place where love comes into creation, where this energy of love begins to flow. It is an energy, a power, the Source of life. And there is no person, not even the drama of lover and Beloved that is so central to the Sufis. Out of the darkness comes this energy.

At the beginning when you first experience it, it is dark, it is the same color as the nothingness out of which it comes. It is so pure, so fine it has no color of its own. Then it comes into creation and there is this extraordinary moment as it enters the planes of creation and there are these rainbow colors of love, all the different qualities of love that we can relate to in this world.

"The One Quality Needed for the Path"

Most live the story of their ego, experienced through the senses and the mind. A story of desires, successes and failures, as well as the complex web of human relationships. The soul's story is different, has different colors, is more meaningful and richer in texture. It tells another story, bonded both to the land and the heart, and is often a journey of self-discovery, as one is drawn deeper within oneself.

"Walking Between Worlds"

The Sufi path is subversive rather than confrontational. It works from within, from the Self which lives in the very depths of the unconscious, in the secret recesses of the heart. The changes begin far away from the conscious mind, where they cannot be interfered with. Then slowly the energy of the Self filters into consciousness, where it begins the work of altering our thinking processes.

Catching the Thread: Sufism, Dreamwork and Jungian Psychology

We are each the human face, the human story of the Divine. One of the greatest gifts of the Earth is to enable us to live this story, to have this experience. In some ways this is also our greatest offering to the Earth, our own unique story, the spark within the heart meeting the light within creation. And in this meeting something comes alive; an unnamable, unknowable Essence takes on form, receives a heartbeat and a breath. It is said that when this moment is made conscious a star is born.

"Walking Between Worlds"

At the beginning we have to learn the art of listening, the art of being present, attentive, and empty. We have to learn to catch the still, small voice from within. We have to learn to be silent, because listening is born from silence. But the listening of the heart is always an act of love, a coming together, even when nothing is heard. Listening is a wisdom so easily overlooked, because it is feminine, receptive, hidden, and our culture values only what is visible. But Rumi knew how central a part it plays in our loving, in our wordless relationship with our Beloved:

> "Make everything in you an ear, each atom of your being, and you will hear at every moment what the Source is whispering to you."

The Circle of Love

Listening is an essential quality of receptivity. We need to learn to listen, to be inwardly and outwardly attentive, watching the signs that tell the real story of life. In our present masculine culture we are often too busy to listen to what life and the Beloved are trying to tell us. Instead we are caught in superficial experiences, and so we miss the meaning, the real purpose of our soul's life. Life is a direct expression of the Divine, but unless we listen to this hidden presence, we experience only the distortions of our ego-self, its desires and anxieties. Life and the soul are always beckoning us, wanting to share the real wonder of being alive.

THE RETURN OF THE FEMININE AND THE WORLD SOUL

We pray to our Beloved who answers us. Knowing that our prayers are heard, we feel the wonder of experiencing that the inner connection of the soul to God exists, not just as an abstract idea, but as a living reality. Being told that God cares for us is very different from experiencing the intimacy and individual nature of this care. The response to our prayers brings into our consciousness, into our daily life, the soul's link to its Beloved. We then no longer believe in God, we *know*.

PRAYER OF THE HEART IN CHRISTIAN AND SUFI MYSTICISM

The substance of spiritual transformation is in the very cellular structure of life. It has to do with the way energy forms into matter. The transformation of energy into matter is one of the mysteries of creation. It is a continual process in which the invisible comes into form. Particle physics has shown us that the world of matter is not as it appears, but is a constantly changing dance of probability. Energy and matter are different images of the same reality. But there is a dynamic of transition when energy takes on form. This is part of the wonder of revelation, the instant in which the invisible presence of the Divine becomes visible.

LIGHT OF ONENESS

Scientists may tell us that our universe began thirteen billion years ago with the Big Bang, when from an infinitely hot and dense single point matter came into existence. But mystics know a different truth: how from the unborn and undying emptiness, existence is constantly being created as a flow of light and love that then becomes physical form. And this love remains, the foundation, the essence of everything—every particle and every star. It is the primary energy, power, presence within the created world. And it is our divine nature, always evolving and changing within our body and soul, even as it remains constant....

Flowing out of the emptiness love is the invisible foundation of creation, present in all of life, in the hummingbird drinking nectar, in the laughter and tears of a child. But in the unborn and undying emptiness before and after creation it cannot be named. This is the depth of the mystical journey in God of which little can be said, even as it is known within the heart.

"LOVER AND BELOVED: MYSTICAL LOVE IN SUFISM"

In the depths of nonbeing there is a light, and this light contains the consciousness of the whole of humanity. This light continually flows into life, determining the development of our consciousness and the patterns of our evolution, giving meaning to each moment in time.

LIGHT OF ONENESS

The development of consciousness has given us the sense of a separate self, but the next stage of this development is to realize the greater oneness of which our individual self is an expression.

LIGHT OF ONENESS

... the light of oneness is available to all of us, present in hidden aquifers where life's waters continue to flow, waiting in a living silence for us to notice.

FOR LOVE OF THE REAL: A STORY
OF LIFE'S MYSTICAL SECRET

There are so many ways to pray for creation, to listen within and include the Earth in our practice. Watching the simple wonder of a dawn can be a prayer in itself. Or when we hear the chorus of birds in the morning we may sense that deeper joy of life and awake to its divine nature. At night the stars can remind us of what is infinite and eternal within us and within the world. Whatever way we are drawn to wonder or pray, what matters is always the attitude we bring to this intimate exchange: whether our prayers are heartfelt rather than just a mental exercise. It is always through the heart that our prayers are heard, even if we first make the connection in our feet or hands. Do we really feel the suffering of the Earth, sense Its need? Do we feel this connection with creation, how we are a part of this beautiful and suffering being? Then our prayers are alive, a living stream that flows from our heart. Then every step, every touch, will be a prayer for the Earth, a remembrance of what is sacred. We are a part of the Earth calling to its Creator, crying in its time of need.

PRAYER OF THE HEART IN CHRISTIAN AND SUFI MYSTICISM

The light within the Earth, what the alchemists called the *lumen naturae*, is a primal source of energy and power that has yet to be fully accessed by humanity. It belongs to our natural relationship to life, to creation and its sacred nature. This energy source can once again become accessible as humanity remembers its place in the whole and relates to all life with an understanding of oneness—of unity and multidimensional interdependence. We cannot work with the Earth's light, nor will we know the real names of creation, through a consciousness of separation or duality. We need to claim the consciousness of oneness that is waiting for us.

FOR LOVE OF THE REAL: A STORY OF LIFE'S MYSTICAL SECRET

We have separated matter and spirit and through the power of this collective attitude have starved the world.

AWAKENING THE WORLD: A GLOBAL DIMENSION TO SPIRITUAL PRACTICE

We need a new story, a story that reconnects us to the Earth and Her sacred nature, and knows how we are interconnected. And this primary connection is Love.

"THREADS OF LOVE"

# 4

# ONENESS

*For those who are awake the Cosmos is one.*

HERACLITUS

Oneness is very simple: everything is included and allowed to live according to its true nature. This is the secret that is being revealed.

Working with Oneness

There is a love that is at the core of creation, a love that is born of oneness and carries the sacred interrelationship of all life. This love is alive within the hearts of those who love the Source of all life; its music is the song of the soul and the hidden purpose of creation. There is a wonder in this love, as well as a terror and beauty. Its wonder and terror come from its unconstricted nature, its limitless freedom; its beauty is a reflection of the face of God.

The Signs of God

Nothing is excluded and the unique nature of every aspect of creation is celebrated. This is how oneness works when it is not just a concept but a living presence. Many patterns and attachments that we think are essential to life will fall away, just as our present structures of power will become redundant. And the wonder of this change is that it need not be gradual, because it belongs to the *now*. Any real change is always a miracle—it happens through the grace of God.

Spiritual Power: How It Works

My own story has been a journey of love. Sitting at the feet of my teacher I experienced a love that was all-embracing, and which took me on its path, back to the Beloved and also into life. Half a century later a new quality of love has emerged, simple and most ordinary, a living light in the web of creation which stretches to the stars and beyond. And because love belongs to oneness, I know that this love is found within the heart and within the cells of everything that exists as well as the primal emptiness I experience in deep meditation. It is my own story and also my gift to life, to the Earth, to the heart of the world.

"My Own Story: A Return to Love"

Facing our darkness we struggle towards the light. Finally, worn away by the conflict the ego surrenders and we are taken beyond these opposites. Just as we first awoke to the pain of separation and the darkness of the lover's imperfection, so do we awaken to the higher consciousness of the Self that experiences the oneness in everything.

The Bond with the Beloved: The Mystical Relationship of Lover and Beloved

We think that the problems of the world and of ourselves can only be solved through "doing," not realizing that it is this focus on ceaseless activity that has created much of our present imbalance. Rather than always asking, "What should I do?" we can learn to reflect, "How should I be?"

THE RETURN OF THE FEMININE AND WORLD SOUL

Oneness is not a metaphysical idea but something so simple and ordinary. It is in every breath, in the wingbeat of every butterfly, in every piece of garbage left in the city streets. This oneness is life, life no longer experienced solely through the fragmented vision of the ego, but known within the heart, felt in the soul. This oneness is the heartbeat of life. It is creation's recognition of its Creator. In this oneness life celebrates itself and its divine origin.

THE RETURN OF THE FEMININE AND WORLD SOUL

All of life is woven together in an endlessly flowing web of energy. Spiritual traditions have always recognized the truth of interdependence, the essential interconnectedness of all existence. Separation is an illusion; all things connect together within a greater wholeness.

LIGHT OF ONENESS

“I was a Hidden Treasure. I longed to be known so I created the world.” From the unknowable oneness are born the myriad wonders of the creation. What is visible reflects what is invisible. The creation in all its beauty and violence reflects the primordial oneness of the Creator. In the creation the Divine makes Itself known to Itself: “None knows God but God.” The purpose of creation is to reveal the Hidden Treasure that we call God. This purpose is held like a seed or embryo within every particle of creation. Nature is the first book of divine revelation.

Just as a sunflower follows the sun so does each particle of creation inwardly turn towards the Creator. Each particle unconsciously knows its Creator and thus embodies the purpose of its creation; in Henry Vaughan’s words, “Each bush and oak doth know I AM.” This knowing is the innermost song of everything that is created. It is creation’s song of praise to the Creator.

IN THE COMPANY OF FRIENDS:
DREAMWORK WITHIN A SUFI GROUP

Time speaks in many voices, many different images and sounds. For the Neolithic builders of Stonehenge, sacred time was marked by the Summer and Winter solstices, particularly the Winter solstice, when, at around 3:50pm the midwinter sun would set in the southwest and its rays flood through the center of the monument, dropping down onto the altar stone. Thousands of years later, for the medieval farmer, time was the changing seasons and the saint's days, as well as the monastery bells ringing out over the fields, marking the monk's daily times for prayer, from matins to vespers.

Today we have atomic clocks that have an expected error of only one second in about 100 million years, but have little relationship to sacred time. For most of us time is no longer cyclical, but rushes us through the days, an ever-passing flow of moments and events.

"Sacred Time"

To recognize the wholeness of life, and how each part belongs to this constantly evolving and changing unity, is a quality of perception we need to have in order to step into the future. This is a way of seeing we need for our journey to continue ...

"Living Oneness"

We are not separate but an integral part of the web of life, which is why we should not fight nature but find a way to cooperate, to work together with each other and the world around us.

"The Natural Order of Things"

There are many ways to experience and participate in this living oneness. But if I have learned anything after half a century of spiritual practice, it is the power of love. Love comes in so many forms and expressions. There are the simple acts of loving kindness towards friends and family, members of our community, or strangers. Love reaches across boundaries, expressing what is most essential and human: what unites rather than divides. "Small things with great love," are more potent and powerful than we realize, because they reconnect us with the spiritual roots of life and its transformative and healing energies. Because life is an expression of love, each act of love is a participation and gift to the whole.

"UNITY AND THE POWER OF LOVE"

... the first step is to acknowledge that the world is a spiritual being. Just as you acknowledge for yourself, that you are a spiritual being. And then there is this mysterious relationship between the individual and the world, which is what has traditionally been known as microcosm and macrocosm—that every human being is the microcosm of the whole.

"INVOKING THE WORLD SOUL"

To be aware of the divine within oneself and the divine within life and the world, and to know that it is all one, is a simple and powerful practice. It means to be present in life as it is—not as one would want it to be. And it means to live in the moment—there can be no transformation in the images of the past or the dreams of the future. Yet we are conditioned to look to the past and the future, rather than daring to live in the now. But only in the now can we participate in the creative mystery of life.

THE RETURN OF THE FEMININE AND THE WORLD SOUL

A consciousness of oneness, an awareness of the unity of life, is the next stage in our collective evolution.

LIGHT OF ONENESS

Every era has its dream. At this time when an old era is dying and a new one being born, it is up to each of us to take conscious responsibility for the images of oneness that are now emerging from the symbolic depths. These images will shape the dream of the new era. Our participation will determine how these images come into being and whether they will take us out of the current nightmare of greed and separatist fanaticism that is destroying our planet and causing such suffering to so many, and into a new way of living with the Earth. They can give us hope, a vision of wholeness, and sustain us with the energy and meaning we need to co-create a new world.

ALCHEMY OF LIGHT: WORKING WITH
THE PRIMAL ENERGIES OF LIFE

At the beginning of every era a spark is given to humanity to help it to evolve, and with this spark is given the energy needed for this unfolding. The spark of the next era is already present: it has a quality of love and unity that expresses itself as global awareness and a deepening care and responsibility for the whole of life and the Earth—"care for our common home."

SPIRITUAL POWER: HOW IT WORKS

One of the most pressing needs of the time is to unify the apparent opposites of spirit and matter. This will enable the magic inherent in matter, the spiritual potential of matter, to awaken and help change the world. But this can only happen through a consciousness of oneness.

LIGHT OF ONENESS

Oneness is a foundational principle for the new era, but in order to recognize how we are a part of this living wholeness we need a new quality of perception, less rigid and more fluid. We need to become more aware of the patterns of interconnection that link together the biosphere, and also the worlds of magic and sacred meaning.

"LIVING ONENESS"

The new story of an awakening Earth is a story of oneness, the oneness of all of creation, which includes not only the webs of dew in an early summer morning, the laughter of children, the tears of lovers, but also all the subtle worlds, the spirits and angels, the names of God, and the masters of wisdom. We are all part of a living, magical wholeness, bonded together in love. We are the vast ocean and the blade of grass. We are the drunkard staggering home at night and the child waiting for the school bus. And we are our own ordinary self, feeling better after a cup of coffee in the morning. And we are also the world waiting before dawn, tired of the darkness, needing the light of the souls of lovers to awaken.

INCLUDING THE EARTH IN OUR PRAYERS:
A GLOBAL DIMENSION TO SPIRITUAL PRACTICE

We are still focused on the old paradigm of treating problems in isolation, as if they existed separate from the whole web of conditions around them. But the problem *is* the isolation we have imposed on ourselves and our world, *is* our myth of separation. Only when we abandon this paradigm and step into an awareness of life's interconnected oneness can the energy of life teach us how to work with it, reconnect our individual consciousness with its primal energy and enable a real alchemy of transformation to take place.

ALCHEMY OF LIGHT: WORKING WITH
THE PRIMAL ENERGIES OF LIFE

This world is starving. Through our collective attitude we are isolating the outer world from its spiritual core. Our focus on materialism, our denial of the sacred within creation, has alienated us from the Source of life. The river of life no longer runs pure—its water is polluted outwardly and inwardly. The symbolic worlds that traditionally connected the outer life with the meaning and sacred nourishment that come from within have been desecrated. The separation from the sacred and the Source is denying life an essential ingredient, a quality of spirit.

For Love of the Real: A Story of Life's Mystical Secret

Everything that is created comes from the inner worlds. The energy of life flows from the uncreated emptiness out into the planes of manifestation. This is why events first constellate on the inner planes. As the energy of life comes into manifestation, it becomes more visible. At first it takes form as a pattern of energy, a fluid, dynamically flowing reality out of which the primal oneness of creation begins to differentiate itself. This is the archetypal dimension where undifferentiated energy constellates into the forms behind the physical world. Finally the energy of creation enters the physical plane and becomes part of the world of the senses, at which time it becomes fixed into matter, into a physical form or event.

Working with Oneness

When we really listen we find ourselves present in another world full of meaning and magic. Then the signs within our outer life and in our dreams can speak to us, and take us on a journey far beyond the limited world of the ego. They open a door to the symbolic world that is just beneath the surface. It is from this inner dimension of images and symbols that the soul is nourished. Recognizing and working with symbols requires an attitude of receptivity that allows the symbols to communicate in their own language. We come to know this ancient part of ourselves that is fully alive and knows the deeper destiny of our soul. And it is from this inner world that our everyday life too is nourished and we are given the direction we need.

The Return of the Feminine and the World Soul

When we work together with life as a living divine wholeness we will see the simple answers life has for sustaining itself.

Darkening of the Light:<br>Witnessing the End of an Era

We cannot afford the stillbirth of new ideas that lack the life force that comes from the depths. We are called to return to the root of our being where the sacred is born. Then, standing in both the inner and outer worlds, we will find our self to be part of the momentous synchronicity of life giving birth to itself.

"Changing the Story"

Unity holds the essential vision that we are one living, interconnected ecosystem—a living Earth that supports and nourishes all of its inhabitants. If we acknowledge and honor this simple reality, we can begin to participate in the vital work of healing our fractured and divisive world and embrace a consciousness of oneness that is our human heritage. This is the opportunity that is being offered to us, even as its dark twin is constellating the dynamics of nationalism, tribalism, isolationism, and all the other regressive forces that express "me" rather than "we."

"Unity and the Power of Love"

Oneness is not an idea, oneness is a life force.

Source Unknown

# 5

# SPIRITUAL ECOLOGY

*Every day, priests minutely examine the Law and endlessly chant complicated sutras. Before doing that, though, they should learn how to read the love letters sent by the wind and rain, the snow and moon.*

IKKYU

Spiritual Ecology is a recognition that at the root of our present ecological crisis is a spiritual crisis, and that the essence of this spiritual crisis is a forgetfulness of the sacred nature of creation. Our present civilization has become separated from the story of the sacred that belongs to the Earth and our shared existence, that is at the foundation of life itself. As a result we have come to see the Earth as a resource to be exploited and polluted, existing to serve our materialist values, rather than a living being to revere and respect. The work of spiritual ecology is to reconnect with the sacred, so that we can return to a way of life that is in balance with the Earth.

SEASONS OF THE SACRED: RECONNECTING TO THE WISDOM WITHIN NATURE AND THE SOUL

How can we speak about sustainability without speaking about the Sustainer?

"SPIRITUAL ECOLOGY"

There was a time when every grove and stream was sacred, meaning and wisdom were found in the cycles of the moon and the germination of the plants. The Divine was seen as present in everything, from the fire on the hearth to the stars in the heavens. The Earth was marked by lines of power, called "ley lines" in the West, "dragon lines" in the East. Where certain lines intersected, temples and circles of standing stones were built. These were places of power where spiritual energy was most concentrated and accessible. The power at these sites and their temples not only helped people in their relationship to the Divine, but also aided the flow of spiritual energy into the whole of life. Through these places of power, nature was nourished, the crops grew, and the people benefited both inwardly and outwardly, in their souls and in their daily lives.

Spiritual Power: How It Works

So much was given at this time, when the soul of humanity and the soul of the world were bonded together, and the Earth showed Her generosity. The land was pristine and its sacred nature known and praised. It was a time of beginning, the time of the Original Instructions, when the servants of light began their work of awakening the world. It was then that the sacred names of creation were first given to human beings. First to the shamans, healers and keepers of the sacred ways—the names of animals that evoked their power, the names of plants that revealed their healing properties, the names of rivers and mountains that ensured that the world was kept in harmony and balance—and through them humanity and the created world came into a new relationship and sang together. There was a purity of intention in this relationship between humanity and the Earth and all of its myriad creatures; their partnership had a sacred purpose. Together they would work to awaken the magic and light hidden within the physical world,[3] and that light would serve a higher purpose. This was the beginning of the covenant between humanity and creation—how the natural world was the first book of divine revelation.

"A Story of Beginnings: A Personal Story of Memories of Magic and Wonder"

There was a time, long ago, when all of the multiplicity of creation was named for the first time. Through the power of its names, creation came alive to its higher purpose. Each thing that was named, each flower and tree, each animal and insect, became conscious of its true nature and purpose in the web of creation. This knowing, quite different from conscious knowing as we understand it today, is rather an instinctual, innate knowing belonging more to the spirit of each life-form. Through it, the world came alive with the magic of naming.

The sacred names of creation were also used to make a relationship between humanity and the created world. Every plant, every animal on Earth had a name, and humanity knew these names. The names of animals evoked their power, the names of plants revealed their healing properties, the names of rivers and mountains ensured that the world was kept in harmony and balance. Humanity's knowing of the power and purpose of Earth awakened Earth to its own power, its magic and sacred meaning.[4]

For Love of the Real: A Story
of Life's Mystical Secret

In this primordial time, the power of the Word, the *logos* principle, and the names of creation brought light and consciousness into creation. It was the awakening of the Earth, when after millions of years of unconsciousness, the world began to know its purpose as an expression of God, and each created thing began to awaken to its unique expression of sacredness ...

For Love of the Real: A Story
of Life's Mystical Secret

If we are to become partners with the Earth, living our shared journey, we have to once again speak the same language, listen with our senses attuned not just to the physical world, but also to its inner dimension.

"Where the Horses Sing"

The world is not a problem to be solved; it is a living being to which we belong. The world is part of our own self and we are a part of its suffering wholeness. Until we go to the root of our image of separateness, there can be no healing. And the deepest part of our separateness from creation lies in our forgetfulness of its sacred nature, which is also our own sacred nature.

Spiritual Ecology:
The Cry of the Earth

At this present time, when the story of humanity and its patterns of conquest and control are in direct conflict with the story of the Earth and its patterns of biodiversity, how can we find our way back to the living Earth?

"The Space Between Stories"

Our separation from the natural world may have given us the fruits of technology and science, but it has left us bereft of any instinctual connection to the spiritual dimension of life—the connection between our soul and the soul of the world, the knowing that we are all part of one living, spiritual being.

SPIRITUAL ECOLOGY:
THE CRY OF THE EARTH

We live in a civilization whose materialistic values and total reliance on rationality have denied even the existence of the inner reality that underlies all of creation, whose energies form the "river beds of life."

FOR LOVE OF THE REAL: A STORY
OF LIFE'S MYSTICAL SECRET

By "developing" the planet, we have been reducing Earth to a new type of barrenness.

SPIRITUAL ECOLOGY:
THE CRY OF THE EARTH

The fact that we have to fight for something so essential to life as the integrity of seeds, speaks to the real drama of this present time: that we have to preserve what is most fundamental and sacred to life.

SACRED SEED: A COLLECTION OF ESSAYS

We are all part of one living being we call the Earth, magical beyond our understanding. She gives us life and Her wonder nourishes us. In Her being the worlds come together. Her seeds give us both bread and stories. For centuries the stories of seeds were central to humanity, myths told again and again—stories of rebirth, life recreating itself in the darkness. Now we have almost forgotten these stories. Instead, stranded in our separate, isolated selves we do not even know how hungry we have become. We have to find a way to reconnect with what is essential—to learn once again how to walk in a sacred manner, how to cook with love and prayers, how to give attention to simple things. We need to learn to welcome life in all its colors and fragrances, to say "yes" again and again. Then life will give us back the connection to our own soul, and once more we will hear its song. Then meaning will return as a gift and a promise. And something within our own heart will open and know that we have come home.

"Meaning and the Song of the Soul"

First we have to step out of our dream of separation, the insularity with which we have imprisoned ourselves, and acknowledge that we are a part of a multidimensional living spiritual being we call the world. The world is much more than just the physical world we perceive through the senses, just as we are much more than just our own physical bodies. Only as a part of a living whole can we help to heal the whole. Just as we need to work together with the outer ecosystem, we need to work together with the inner worlds. We need their support and help, their power and knowledge. The nature *devas* understand the patterns of climate change better than we do, because they are the forces behind the weather and the winds. Just as plant *devas* know the healing powers of plants (and taught the shamans and healers their knowledge), so are there more powerful *devas* that know and guide the patterns of evolution of the whole planet.

"SPIRITUAL ECOLOGY"

The "sacred" is not something primarily religious or even spiritual. It is not a quality we need to learn or to develop. It belongs to the primary nature of all that is. When the First Peoples felt that everything they saw was sacred, this was not something taught but instinctively known. It was as natural as sunlight, as necessary as breathing. We all have within us a sense of the sacred, a sense of reverence, however we may articulate it. It is a part of our human nature.

"SEASONS OF THE SACRED: SACRED TIME"

If we remember the sacred we will find ourself in a world as whole as it is holy. However we may call this mystery it permeates all of creation. It may be more easily felt in certain places—in ancient groves, beneath star-filled skies, in temples or cathedrals, in the chords of music. But this is a mystery that belongs to all that exists—there is nothing that is separate from it.

"The Magic of Creation"

We each carry this primal knowing within our consciousness, even if we have forgotten it. A relationship to the sacred is older than any formalized religion, even though it lies at the foundation of many religions. It is a fundamental recognition of the wonder, beauty, and divine nature of the world. It is a felt reverence, an inner sense ...

Seasons of the Sacred: Reconnecting to the Wisdom Within Nature and the Soul

Like the cells of our body, all of life is in constant communication, as science is just beginning to understand. No bird sings in isolation, no bud breaks open alone. And the most central note that is present in life is its sacred nature, something we need to each rediscover and honor anew. We need to learn once again how to walk and breathe in a sacred universe, to feel this heartbeat of life. Hearing its presence speak to us, we feel this great bond of life that supports and nourishes us all. Today's world may still at times make us feel lonely, but we can then remember what every animal, every insect, every plant knows—and only we have forgotten: the living sacred whole.

"Loneliness and the Sacred Web of Life"

Spring is the time of birth and beginnings, from the first shoot pushing up through the softening earth, the first bud breaking into blossom, and the first stirrings of the soul awakening to its true nature. Love also has a springtime, the turning within the heart as heart looks for heart, lover for beloved. The energy of life and love flow through everything, and Spring is the time when it begins to be reborn, to surface from the sleep of Winter.

There is a deep joy in this awakening, the joy that belongs to life itself—life that is sacred.

Seasons of the Sacred: Reconnecting to the Wisdom Within Nature and the Soul

And just as in our inner relationship with the Beloved we learn to be silent and receptive to love's voice, we have to let life speak to us. We need to recognize that life is a constant communion between lover and Beloved. Each moment love is speaking to us in a thousand voices, which are also one voice.

Spiritual Power: How It Works

One of my favorite practices, or prayer, is to imagine placing the world within my heart and feel the love that infuses everything—every bird and butterfly, the trees and the ocean, the chipmunks that have just reappeared in the garden after their hibernation, the bleary-eyed child waiting for the school bus I pass on my morning walk. Everything, every dream, every cloud passing, is infused with love, is an expression of love. Love is the Source of all that exists, *is* all that exists. This primary mystical awareness is stamped into my soul and consciousness, following me throughout the day, and especially in the early hours of the morning, when prayer takes me, when the world of thoughts has faded away and the heart's presence is all that matters.

"Love and Prayer"

This journey has taken me from formlessness to form, to life's unending multiplicity, beautiful, numinous, and most ordinary. And then back into the infinite emptiness of the beyond. Love cries and often my heart feels broken. I sense that love is really all we have to give, and the meaning behind every experience that touches the soul. Love is life's greatest gift and our greatest gift back to life. And especially at this time, life, the Earth, is calling out to be loved, to be held in the heart, so that this thread of love that is present throughout creation can support it in its crisis, so that a new story for humanity and the Earth can begin to be woven into the fabric of existence.

"Love and Prayer"

Through our love for the Earth we will have access to a deeper dimension of our own nature, a living heritage that can nourish us with the meaning and magic that comes from our soul and the world soul. We will also discover ancient forces within creation that can help free us from the spell of consumerism, from its entrancement.

"Global Citizens of a Living Earth"

Love and care are what calls us.... It is our love for the Earth that will heal what we have desecrated, that will guide us through this wasteland, helping our dying Earth to regenerate, and help us to bring light back into our darkening world. Love links us all together in the most mysterious ways, and love can guide our hearts and hands. The central note of love is oneness. Love speaks the language of oneness, of unity rather than separation.

Including the Earth in Our Prayers:
A Global Dimension to Spiritual Practice

There was a time when the language of the Earth was the language of our daily lives, of planting and harvesting, sunshine and storms. The words of the sacred were stars and seeds, mountains and rivers. The soul and the seasons of nature moved together; they spoke the same mystery, the beauty that is within and around us. It was all as natural as breathing, not needing to be remembered because never forgotten. How could you forget the wind on your face or the songs of birds? How could you forget the rise and fall of the tide? These were not stories written in books but lived from morning until dusk, until dreamtime wove another texture into the firelight.

Seasons of the Sacred: Reconnecting to the
Wisdom Within Nature and the Soul

... the sacred principles of life have never been written down: they belong to the heartbeat, to the rhythm of the breath and the flow of blood. They are alive like the rain and the rivers, the waxing and waning of the moon. If we learn to listen we will discover that life, the Great Mother, is speaking to us, telling us what we need to know. We are present at a time when the world is dying and waiting to be reborn, and all the words in our libraries and on the Internet will not tell us what to do. But the sacred feminine can share with us her secrets, tell us how to be, how to midwife her rebirth. And because we are her children she can speak to each of us, if we have the humility to listen.

THE RETURN OF THE FEMININE AND THE WORLD SOUL

Grief opens our heart to love, and it is our love for the Earth that can heal what has been abused and desecrated.

"A FOUR-POINT PLAN REVISITED"

Many people now use the term "climate grief" to describe the many losses in our present world, changes that have happened or are yet to come. There is the personal grief experienced, for example, when a place of beauty or a wild habitat known in one's childhood has vanished, but also the collective grief for how we are treating this beautiful, suffering world; how, for example, the vast landscapes of monoculture and use of pesticides have torn at the web of life and all its patterns of biodiversity. And often if the grief is not recognized or accepted, it can lead to anxiety, also known as "eco-anxiety." But if this grief is recognized, this sorrow accepted, it can take us deeper within, back to our love for the Earth. And the Earth needs our love, as much as it needs our recognition of its suffering.

"A Four-Point Plan Revisited"

I firmly believe that evolution is not just "natural selection," which in my mind is too simplistic and mechanical to include the fully animate world in which we belong. Rather the way plants and animals have changed and adapted over the millennia embodies the intelligence within nature. All of nature has its own spirit intelligence that adapts to the changing patterns of creation, forming the interdependent patterns that we are now beginning to recognize—how, for example, a fungus deep within the jungle communicates to ants what leaves from specific trees it needs to nourish it. The natural world is alive with its own intelligence, which Indigenous People always recognized and could understand and listen, speak its language. Today we have so many words but so few ways to communicate with the world around us. And if we are to find our way out of the present ecological devastation, we need more than ever to communicate with nature so we can work together towards a living future. So that once again we can rejoin the Great Conversation, of which the elemental natural world is our true partner. Sadly, in most present environmental discussions we are still only talking to ourselves.

"Angels and Devas"

Years ago I had a series of visions of the future, of a civilization waiting to be born. I was shown how we would find new ways of healing, bringing together the wisdom of the shaman with the techniques of modern medicine. I saw how we would be given a technology as simple as photosynthesis that could provide us all with free and unpolluting energy from the sun. I saw earth magic coming alive, plants speaking to us again after centuries of silence. But I did not see how we would transition: the hard broken road we would have to travel, what we now call climate crisis and social breakdown, the unraveling caused by our present unsustainable way of life. Visions are often simple and clear, full of light and love, and lack the messiness of everyday. I did not see the farmers leaving their cracked and barren land, the camps of refugees, migrants fleeing hunger and violence, sometimes being sold into prostitution. I still do not see how this present civilization will finally break apart and die, become just a shattered monument to a people who have lost their way. But I hold true to the magic of those visions, and I also sense how many of today's stories, especially the distortions of social media, will be lost as the waters rise.

"Fire Season"

The foundations of life are shifting; the patterns of creation are in the process of being reformed. In this time of transition, forces from the unknown will permeate our life with both danger and opportunity. There is need for extreme attentiveness.

Spiritual Power: How It Works

There is a pressing need to heal ourselves and the Earth—a call to return to a place of reverence, a way of living that honors life and all of its inhabitants. But first we need to rest in our busy lives and find silence.

"7 Days of Rest: A Time to Heal"

Silence draws us inward, away from the clutter and distractions of our outer life, to the deeper roots of our being. Here our soul nourishes us, here we can be replenished, and here we can help replenish our world.

"A Time for Silence"

Life is a self-sustaining organic whole of which we are a part, and once we reconnect with this whole we can find a different way to live—one that is not based upon a need for continual distraction and the illusions of material fulfillment, but rather a way to live that is sustaining for the whole.

"Global Citizens of a Living Earth"

The awareness of the sacred reconnects our consciousness to the primal structure of life ...

"Sustainability, Deep Ecology, and the Sacred"

Always there is this primary place of belonging in the land and in our souls. It used to be a part of the way we lived, how we walked and breathed. Crossing oceans and continents, we carried it with us, a lodestone for our existence. For thousands and thousands of years, it was an essential part of us, never forgotten, because how could you forget the feel of the rain on your skin, or the sound of water flowing over stones? How could you forget the stories and songs passed down through the generations? It is only very recently in our human history—only a few hundred years amidst thousands—that we forgot, that we lost this thread, that our mind ceased to be a part of both the land and the unseen worlds, that we forgot that everything we can see and touch is sacred, and in our forgetting no longer inhabited a world in which everything was alive with spirit, the wind and the rain, the plants and animals.

"Where the Horses Sing"

The patterns of power within the Earth are an ancient secret, part of the knowledge we have lost over the centuries. As we have blinkered our consciousness into seeing only the outer appearances of the material world, we have lost our understanding of its inner, hidden dimensions. Our ideas, beliefs, and attitudes have silenced the song of the Earth and closed the door on Her light.

For Love of the Real: A Story of Life's Mystical Secret

The Earth is calling to us to realize Its essential unity—that She is not a resource to be exploited but a living being crying out for our attention. We are needed to help life to awaken from a dream that is destroying it. But if we are to live the real potential of our spiritual practice, we need to break free from the focus on our own individual journey. We need to reclaim the simple truth that spiritual life is not solely about ourself, and open to a larger, all-embracing vision. If spiritual life is not about the whole, it has lost its true nature; it has instead been subverted by the ego and its patterns of self-concern. Everything that has been created is in service to life, to the real purpose of creation. This belongs to the Original Instructions that were given to the earliest wisdom keepers. We are not separate from each other or from the Earth, and we need to recognize how our individual spiritual journey, our praise and thanksgiving, are part of life's sacred purpose and can nourish life in different ways.

"INCLUDING THE EARTH IN OUR PRAYERS: SPIRITUAL PRACTICE AS A CATALYST FOR CHANGE"

There is action to be taken in the outer world, but it must be action that comes from a reconnection to the sacred—otherwise we will just be reconstellating the patterns that have created this imbalance.

"THE CALL OF THE EARTH"

Walking in a sacred manner is making a connection between your step and the heartbeat of the world.

... when I first started to meditate I also needed to walk. It was not taught or learned, but came as a need, a way to be, an antidote to much of the world around me—a world of people and problems, demands and desires. When one foot follows the other and the day has hardly begun, it seems these demands cannot touch me, as if I am immersed in something simpler, more essential. Placing each foot on the earth is a practice, but a practice that comes from my own roots, not a book or a teacher. Later I came to hear it called "walking in a sacred manner," and it is sacred, a return to what is sacred. But it also is deeper or more primal than any purpose. Nature speaks to me and I listen. Nature calls and something deep within me responds, and I just need to give it space. I am part of a life far greater than any "me."

SPIRITUAL ECOLOGY: 10 PRACTICES TO
REAWAKEN THE SACRED SUBSTANCE IN LIFE

The sacred can be found in any form: a small stone or a mountain, the first cry of a newborn child and the last gasp of a dying person. It can be present in a loaf of bread, on a table, waiting for a meal, and in the words that bless the meal. The remembrance of the sacred is like a central note within life. Without this remembrance something fundamental to our existence is missing. Our daily life lacks a basic nourishment, a depth of meaning.

"MEANING AND THE SONG OF THE SOUL"

And from within this darkening there arises a cry that we hold the light that is left, the light that is within our self and within the spiritual body of the world. So much has been lost, so much has been desecrated by our endless desires, but those of us who are aware of the sacred need to hold what is left, hold it in our hearts and real awareness. The light of the sacred needs our care and protection. Maybe at some time it will give birth to the child with stars in its eyes, to the future whose seeds are still around us.

Darkening of the Light:<br>Witnessing the End of an Era

But in this moment of darkness, in this winter solstice, when it seems we have missed every opportunity, life is recreating itself anew. We are a part of life, part of this recreation, this realignment, even if our attention is completely distracted, even if our way of life is an agent of terrible destruction and desecration, exterminating species as it pollutes the inner and outer worlds. We are both spirit and matter, and along with all of creation we are being reborn. Distracted by the images on our televisions, computer screens, and now smart phones, we might not know this for generations. We are so busy we do not have time to witness what is really happening. There is so little light left it is hard to see, the noise of our daily life is so loud it is difficult to hear. But the cycles of life and the cosmos, the seasons of the soul and the world soul, continue. And the ancient promises are always kept, the promises between heaven and Earth, the promises that give us real hope and meaning, the promises that our souls can hear, even if our senses and our minds cannot.

Darkening of the Light:<br>Witnessing the End of an Era

# 6

# STORIES FOR A LIVING FUTURE

*These stories are both simple and radical:*
*Simple because they describe what is already around us,*
*the wind in the trees, water flowing over stones.*
*Radical because they point to a fundamentally different*
*quality of consciousness, which belongs to both*
*our distant past and our possible future.*

What are the seeds we need for a new story to come fully alive? Returning to a deep ecology of consciousness we can rediscover the magical awareness that belongs to our essential relationship with the living Earth.

"Seeding the Future"

The only way to change the world is to change the story.

"Changing the Story"

In the last years I have come to see that we are the children of a civilization that has lost its way, that has put financial profit before well-being, and is pathologically destroying its own ecosystem. And unless we find our way back to love, love and care for each other and for the Earth—knowing how we are all a part of one community—all of our efforts will not bring the world into balance. Those of us who have looked through the cracks in our present civilization know that it is dying, that stories of "green economic growth" are just fairy tales—our present way of life is simply unsustainable. We need a new story, a story that reconnects us to the Earth and Her sacred nature, and knows how we are all interconnected. And this primary connection is love.

"Threads of Love"

... many of us now long for a new story, one that will restore reverence to the Earth and reconnect our souls to the sacred within creation, a story that will save our planet. Some have even already begun to articulate such a story: a beautiful and compelling vision of the entire universe as a single, inextricably interconnected, living whole, returning to us a sense of wonder that nourishes our body and soul.

"Changing the Story"

... this is also a new story, arising from deep within the psyche of humanity and the world soul at this moment in our and its evolution. It includes the mystery of life as well as the understanding that science can give us. It is a story of cooperation rather than competition or conflict. We are not the sole creators of this story, because it is the story of life evolving, recreating itself anew, but we are needed to midwife it into existence. As with all births it needs to come from the inner to the outer world.

"Changing the Story"

Over the last years I have written a number of stories about returning our consciousness to the living Earth, a numinous world alive in both matter and spirit. As we travel through the darkening days of the present time there is a primal need to find a pathway back to this landscape, experienced through our senses and our dreams.... These stories are an opportunity to become immersed in this landscape, physical and imaginal, and through this shift in awareness to be able to walk towards a living future.

"Introduction: Stories for a Living Future"

These are stories of the heart, words which belong to the depths of my soul as well as to the empty places I have wandered, the visions I have seen, the beauty and sorrow I have come to know. And always a return to what is simple, which sings with the beauty and wonder of our shared existence.

“Introduction: Stories of the Heart”

Maybe I am just a mystic who has travelled too far in the inner worlds, growing old in a world that knows nothing of these things, one that recognizes only a tangible, physical world, or the strange in-between online world made of ones and zeros, that has devoured so much of our attention in the last decades. Maybe I am just nostalgic for a simpler, lost time, when the hedgerows were full of birds and butterflies and wild plants. But in my journey I have come to see what is essential to our human nature, the light and love that sustains our soul and even the cells of our body, although our science has no knowledge of this. As I have said elsewhere, this world is not as we think; it is made from a substance that is not of atoms or particles, and in its depths there is a hidden song. Maybe at some moments in my life I have touched this substance, caught a line of this song. Maybe I have felt the heart of the world in my dreams, or while walking one still early morning. And in these stories I try to share this experience that life and love have given to me.

“Into the Light and Back Again”

One day, both in the present moment and far from now, words will once again become alive, names will be sacred and sing together with the patterns of creation, its magic and sacred meaning. The inner and outer worlds will no longer be separate but speak to each other, tell secrets. I would like to wait for this language to arrive, but I am too old and this future too far away. So instead I hint of pathways and gardens whose gate is always open, of ways to listen and bear witness.

"Words"

For many Indigenous Peoples their language and place are intimately connected, often conveying a detailed knowledge of the flora, fauna, sacred sites, and songlines of the area. In my own journey I have been drawn to describe a space where the inner and outer worlds meet, a shoreline where dreams come into our lives, where synchronicities happen. I also rediscovered this language in nature, walking the trails near to my home, in the trees and birds, flowers and animals, and how they all spoke to me. If nature is the first book of revelation, here were the stories in this book, like the foxglove flowers opening purple and white, or the bobcat crossing the trail in front of me. They convey the living oneness all around; how we are all part of a more-than-human world that speaks in so many voices, always articulating the same ever-changing mystery we call life.

"A Hidden Pathway"

Nature in both Her beauty and violence is calling us to return, to rejoin the "great conversation" where the wind and the stars still speak to us. As we travel this liminal landscape between stories, between civilizations, and experience the primal insecurity of a civilization unraveling, we need to feel that we belong, not to a political ideology, a race, nation, or some conspiracy theory, but to the living presence that has sustained us for thousands of years, back to when we journeyed as small groups of hunters and gatherers, back to when we spoke the same language as the animals and plants. Then we were awake with all of our senses, with ceremonies and dreams attuned to both the seen and unseen worlds, long before we "settled" the land, and then forgot it was sacred.

"Threads of Love"

I would like to say I live at the still center of the turning world
That from dawn to dusk I spend the day in meditation
And pray through the night,
That I walk with light feet over the high mountain passes.
But here where I live at the edge of the world it is not like this.

"Threads of Love"

My own story has been a journey of love. Sitting at the feet of my teacher I experienced a love that was all-embracing, and which took me on its path, back to the Beloved and also into life. Half a century later a new quality of love has emerged, simple and most ordinary, a living light in the web of creation which stretches to the stars and beyond. And because love belongs to oneness, I know that this love is found within the heart and within the cells of everything that exists as well as the primal emptiness I experience in deep meditation. It is my own story and also my gift to life, to the Earth, to the heart of the world.

"My Own Story: A Return to Love"

Love is the simplest, most direct connection, to each other, to the Earth, and to the Beloved. It should be tasted with our mother's milk and sensed in our earliest relationship to the natural world around. It is in the dawn chorus and the first green shoots of Spring. It is watching a tomato ripen and tasting a freshly picked berry. It is the world our ancestors inhabited, still present in landscapes that have not been lost or polluted. It is pushing a swing in the playground and bedtime stories, and those simple words "I love you."

"My Own Story: A Return to Love"

And love is free, a gift to each of us. Even if it costs blood and a broken heart, it is still free. Love is life speaking to its Beloved and the Beloved speaking to life. And in that conversation so many things can happen, so many miracles can be born—the small unsuspected miracles that we often do not notice, like a moment of sunlight through the clouds, a flower blossoming from the sprout of a seed, a smile from a stranger. This world is steeped in this divine quality that is waiting to be born, to be brought into existence, to be loved into being. And just to be a part of it is enough, is a story that sings in the heart.

"LOVE AND PRAYER"

In the heart of the world the future is being written in the language of love. Our ability to read this language will determine whether we participate creatively in our own destiny and the destiny of the world or whether we are victims of fate, blindly reacting to the events that happen to us....

The language of love is how we interact with life on the most fundamental level. But we have forgotten how to read the signs of life and we have relegated the language of love to our images of romance and personal relationships. We need to return to the primal recognition that creation is an expression of divine love.

SPIRITUAL POWER: HOW IT WORKS

In order to understand more fully the changes taking place I try to let the Earth and my heart speak to me, tell me their story, how the threads of creation are being rewoven into a new pattern. What does it mean that a doorway between the worlds is opening? How can those whose hearts are open become part of a prayer that speaks to the Earth, that welcomes what is being born within Her?

"EARTH CHANGES"

Looking at this world today we see darkness more often than light. The primal song of creation, when the rivers and the mountains touched us with sacred music and meaning, has almost faded away. Instead there are the noise, the pollution, and the distortions of the wasteland we have created with our greed and desires. But this is not how it was in the Original Instructions, the ancient wisdom given to us in the early days.

And those instructions are still present, if we know how to look, how to remember. If we dare to return to this deeply human way to be with the Creator in Her creation, with our feet touching the ground, its magic can come alive again. Then in our praise and thanksgiving the worlds of light and the world of matter come together. We are both heaven and earth, born from stardust and soil. If we can only remember that, the bond of love between the two can once again come alive within our hearts. This is the prayer and the promise that have held me here in this world.

"SEEDING THE FUTURE"

These are all stories of a living Earth long forgotten by our rational selves, and a Western history of spirituality divorced from the physical world. We may know about the magnetic axis of the Earth, but not its spiritual axis, the *axis mundi*, its cosmic axis. The place where the inner and outer worlds meet. Sufis have always known about the axis of love, which belongs to Its spiritual body, how this keeps the worlds aligned....

The axis of love is part of the gift of the earliest masters, who awoke the Earth to its divine nature. This axis spins with the frequency of divine love, and is present within every cell of creation, every plant, every animal, every song. It is the link of love between the Creator and the creation, which the Sufis call *nisbat*. It contains the secret of creation, its divine unity, or the oneness of being, which has been held in the heart, in the mystical consciousness of "the people of the secret," the Sufis and those who came before them....

The lover looks after the axis of love in the world through the simplicity of her devotions, through keeping her heart pure and the attention of the heart turned towards God while she lives her everyday life. How we live the love affair that is creation is unique to each of us. No two ways of love are the same. But every lover lives the same axis of love. It is alive in our hearts, present in each and every breath. And when we remember our Beloved, it sings within us, nourishing life in the most hidden and wonderful ways.

"A New Note in the Axis of Love"

Walking between worlds, between stories, in a landscape where everything is uncertain, requires courage and conviction, a desire to step outside the arid land of our present civilization and its conditioning, even if we still walk its streets, still buy our food in its supermarkets. That is why it is so important to have communities to support us, a simple spiritual practice to anchor us. And if possible to find a place of belonging in a world that is becoming more and more out of balance, at times even appearing increasingly crazy.

"The Gift of a Garden"

And in our hearts there is a seed of a future that returns to the beginning, to when the Source ran free and the names of creation sang in the wind.

"Seeding the Future"

... we can no longer afford to impose ourselves on the living system we call the Earth. We have to learn once again how to listen to the rivers and the wind, to hear the grass growing ... where the sacred speaks to us as it spoke to our elders.

"Listening to the Wind"

A basic spiritual teaching is to live in the present moment, the now. Rather than being caught in our mind's patterns, planning for the future or memories of the past, we are present in the intensity of each moment. In this way we are more fully alive....

In my own experience I have come to discover that what is born from this living moment is a quality of awareness very different to the demands and rigidity of rational consciousness.

"A Hidden Pathway"

Only in the moment is the eternal dimension of the soul present, and also love can only be experienced in the moment. As Rumi says, "Step out of the circle of time and into the circle of love." Love belongs outside of time, which is why it is always forever. The true nature of service can also only be lived when one is fully attentive to the needs of the moment. Only in the moment can one fully participate in life. It is here, in the moment that the stories of the future can be written, or as my own teacher said, "we all work for the future ... but only the moment of now matters."

"A Hidden Pathway"

Watching the breath, watching it rise and fall, come and go, is the simplest way to be present. One cannot breathe in the past or future, and here there are no thoughts, just simple awareness. For some this is an awareness of the body, sensations and feelings. But the breath also has a mystery, long known to spiritual practice. The breath connects together the worlds—the outer world of the senses and the inner world of the soul. With each and every in-breath we return back to our own soul, until the out-breath draws us into the outer world. Mystery upon mystery, with each and every breath.

"THE LIVING MOMENT: REFLECTIONS OF AN OLD MAN"

I know that just as the rising sun and the apples in the orchard speak of seasons and cycles, so too does the Earth Herself. For so many lifetimes I have walked together with Her, listened to Her, watched the sun slip over the hills, turn orange in the sky. Her song belongs to the present moment, but speaks to both the past and the future.

"EARTH CHANGES"

Sometimes dreams link the worlds, or visions show a different landscape to our outer eyes, places where the horses sing. Thinking only in terms of material well-being we miss these signs—our eyes are blind, our ears deaf, our hearts hard. Because we can no longer read the book of life we are stumbling into an unknown future, missing the signs of our belonging, of our homecoming. We have forgotten how the birth of consciousness was also the birth of soul awareness, of an inner world that spoke and sang, that gave us visions and meaning. The first artists who painted spirals on stone knew of this mystery, as did the storytellers and seers. Maybe it is time to recognize the land we have left, the magic abandoned, the wells that never ran dry.

“Living Oneness”

In our naïveté we think that the future of the Earth depends upon humanity. But we are only co-creators of our collective destiny. There are other forces and influences that need to be recognized and included. The Earth Herself has Her own agenda, and there are also forces that come from the beyond. We need to acknowledge that we are a part of an interdependent living organism that contains many different relationships.

Spiritual Power: How It Works

When Skywoman fell to Earth, heaven and Earth were connected. Our human lives were part of a cosmos of sacred meaning. Gods and goddesses spoke to us. Our soul, the world soul, and the stars—microcosm and macrocosm—were not separate. When I was first shown the archetypal changes happening to the Earth, the image of the future that came to me was a child with stars in its eyes. This image has stayed with me for over thirty years, even as our world has become darker and more toxic. It reminds me that the Earth has Her own story, which belongs to humanity but also to dimensions beyond our present understanding. Our journey together with the Earth is taking us through the debris of a civilization causing ecocide, but also reconnecting us with patterns long forgotten, with myths and sacred meaning lost from our rational minds, a landscape which includes the heavens.

"WATCHING THE STARS"

Around us we can see the cascading crises of the end of an era, but we have little awareness of how the Earth Herself is changing. Even as the Earth is suffering, life is recreating itself. There are deep patterns of realignment taking place, patterns that need our cooperation, our co-creation.

"A DREAM OF THE EARTH"

Hopefully this time between eras, this *bardo*, will not be so brutal, but there will be a time of radical insecurity, until maybe in two centuries or more a new civilization may emerge, quite different to now. It will not be known by its monuments, but by its qualities of compassion and kindness, a deep knowing of the oneness that binds us together. And also by its ways of working with the land. It too will have its dark side, but it will no longer exploit the Earth. That is a pain and a suffering humanity will not want to repeat. Some knowledge will be passed down to the future, while new knowledge will be revealed. Each era has its own quality of knowing.

"Watching the Stars"

It is time to rediscover this deeper dimension of our journey together with the Earth, how we are born from both stardust and soil, and how the Earth needs our love and care and attention, our prayers, to come fully alive again. And how this rebirth will be a transformation for both the Earth and humanity. Because we have dismissed the inner worlds, because we no longer believe in magic and think that the human journey is about survival, it is difficult to grasp the meaning of this moment in time when the doors between the worlds stand open, "when the skin between the two worlds opens."

The Earth will change. This is part of the evolving dance of the cosmos. What is less sure is the part we will play in this shift. There are deep patterns of realignment taking place, patterns that need our cooperation, dynamics of co-creation.

"A Dream of the Earth"

Returning to silence, embracing stillness, we can be present in this liminal space. Watching the breath we can be present between the in-breath and the out-breath. Being part of the movement of the breath, the flow of life, we can be both at its source and amidst its many manifestations. That is why, amidst all the many demands of today's world, it is of such value to be able to return to stillness, to be a space where the future can be born, free of the restrictions of the past, not caught in any of the hierarchies or dynamics of power that define so much of our present existence, our civilization and its toxic patterns of behavior. Nor seduced by fantasies of the future. The future will arrive unannounced, part of the miracle of life recreating itself.

"The Space Between Stories"

This is a moment, a decade, that will affect future generations—not just with rising temperatures but with a quality of life that belongs to the soul. We need to walk carefully, with awareness of where we place our feet.

"Watching at the Edge of the World"

One day, far into the future, we will look back on this time with amazement. That we walked so unknowingly into the coming days, that we waited so long, that we hesitated until every opportunity was almost missed. And when the darkness came we did not recognize the signs we had been shown. We did not recognize how the ground under our feet had shifted, how our inner and outer alignment had changed. Not only our awareness, even our dreaming had been censored.

"INTO THE LIGHT AND BACK AGAIN"

Why is the fabric of our society being stretched, almost broken? Why are there places where no birds sing? What stories should be believed and what are born from unlived dreams that rise to the surface and then dissolve again? Sometimes I wonder about our culture that knows so much and has so little knowledge. That can see with a microscope but not with the heart, that has many statistics but so little understanding. Life was always a dance between the inner and outer worlds, known in our dreams and our senses. But now we walk in a world that sees only what is tangible, even as it is caught in endless fantasies and conspiracy theories, and a terrible war born from the myth of a lost empire.

"WATCHING AT THE EDGE OF THE WORLD"

Here, at the edge of the world I watch the waves. And I remember sitting half a century ago in my teacher's small room in North London, fully sensing for the first time the unseen worlds, a place of miracles and the presence of spiritual masters. I wonder how we can have forgotten our spiritual heritage, those masters and beings of light who are here to help us and help the Earth, to help us plant the seeds for a new civilization, a civilization born from oneness and love, that honors our connection to the living Earth. I know that we need to return to what is essential, even as we water these seeds with our tears for how we are betraying the Earth. I know that the spiritual quest is not something separate from life, but woven into the Original Instructions that were given to the earliest wisdom keepers. Meditation, prayer, the mysteries of the heart and the wonder of creation, its beauty and wisdom, are part of a great tapestry that stretches to the stars and beyond. And those of us who belong to love, who care for the Earth, can begin to weave into this tapestry a new thread that contains the colors of the next era, not a broken world full of greed and exploitation, but once again earth magic coming alive as it did on the first day.

And maybe, one day, far into the future, the heart of the world will open and start to sing, as it sang for our ancestors long ago. And in this song we will experience how all the plants and animals, mountains and rivers, birds and butterflies, have their own magic, their own message, and how it is part of one living tapestry of divine love.

"Threads of Love"

… just as stories nourish our soul, give us a sense of belonging, so too do stories nourish the Earth in hidden ways. This is part of the ancient covenant between humanity and the natural world, how magic is woven into the web of life and how that magic can come alive again, in the songlines of Dreamtime, in the images of the First Peoples, spirals engraved on stone, or the animals—bison and bulls, even a rhinoceros—painted on the cave walls. Our rational world may have banished magic from our consciousness, but it is still very present in the Earth and Her ways. It speaks of the hidden mysteries of life, the power of sacred place, or the healing properties of plants. This is traditionally the domain of the priest or shaman, but is also our common heritage, part of the wisdom of the early days. And when we speak to the Earth with reverence and thanksgiving, when our stories are true, then the magic within the world can come alive, and can nourish life, clear the water that has become polluted, return to it powers that have been lost.

"When the Source Ran Free"

And even now, even when thousands of years have passed, civilizations come and gone, even now in this time of the great forgetting—when the wells run dry, when the air is toxic, when we are at the end of an era in the time of the great dying—that essential note is once again present in my consciousness, that song of creation, of what is born and comes into being. Without this return to the Source nothing true can be born, just more layers of distortion, more veils that obscure us from what is Real. And this note of the Source is so simple. It is not an answer to a question, because in the simplicity of Self there is no question. Like a bud breaking open in springtime, it just *is*—life returning after a long winter, after storms and snow.

"When the Source Ran Free"

# 7

# WHERE THE TWO SEAS MEET

*There they found a servant from among Our servants*
*whom We had granted Mercy from Us and*
*whom We had taught knowledge*
*from Our Presence.*

QUR'AN
SURA 18:65

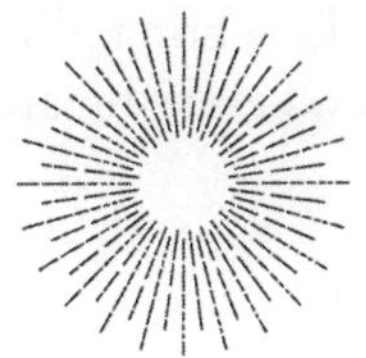

Magic is life awake.

Magic is born between the worlds, where the inner and the outer meet. It is part of the mysterious relationship of the Creator and creation, how the inner flows into life and back again.... When creation remembers its Creator, it brings the joy of the soul into life. The joy of the soul will redeem and heal life at its deepest level. This belongs to the evolutionary shift we are waiting for.[5]

Spiritual Power: How It Works

The unseen world is all around us, helping us, speaking to us through synchronicities and dreams. We belong in the inner worlds, in the wonder of what is hinted at but not yet visible. Our own life is part of a flow of energy from the inner to the outer; every breath follows this rhythm. We are the meeting of the worlds, which is why human beings have the potential to make everything sacred, to bring alive the mystery of divine remembrance in each and every breath.

Spiritual Power: How It Works

Life is a mystery and not a problem. It is a mysterious coming together of the worlds, a continual breathing in and out in which the physical and the dream worlds interpenetrate within us. Walking in both worlds, we are the place where the worlds meet, where the insubstantial takes on form and the physical reveals its foundation in the symbolic. We have both a symbolic and a physical existence, and only when we understand their relationship can we live a grounded and meaningful life.

Alchemy of Light: Working with the Primal Energies of Life

There is a way for a human being to *be* where the worlds come together, where the manifest world is not a dream, not a "dewdrop within a dewdrop," but an expression of the Real.

In the Sufi tradition this is "where the two seas meet," and it is here that we encounter Khidr, the figure of divine revelation.

For Love of the Real: A Story of Life's Mystical Secret

This place where the two seas meet is the locus of the mystical journey.

Fragments of a Love Story: Reflections on the Life of a Mystic

Each breath is an invitation into the oneness of the Absolute. Each breath connects all levels of reality, the inner and the outer. Through the breath, heaven and earth unite.

For Love of the Real: A Story of Life's Mystical Secret

Mystics have gone beyond the clouds to the sky, gone beyond the sky to the spaces between the stars, into the dazzling darkness where the names of God are in potential. And yet we are also here, with our feet on the ground, breathing into life those names, so that the stories of divine love can be written in both worlds.

For Love of the Real: A Story of Life's Mystical Secret

If we go within ourselves, we will find that there is a simple connection between us and the Source of life, a way of being that is part of our very nature in which our spiritual and natural selves align themselves in harmony and nourish each other. It is in our breath, and if we live consciously, it is present in every step we take. This connection is the place in us where the worlds meet.

Alchemy of Light: Working with the Primal Energies of Life

The connections of life are its lifeblood. We are physically nourished by our natural ecosystem, and also by the connections of trade that bring food to our tables. We are emotionally nourished by our family and friends, and sustained in emotional and practical ways by the different types of communication that play an increasingly important part in our life, the cell phone and email that have so quickly become a vital source of connection. The connections of the soul are more hidden in our culture, but are present in our dreams and in our search for meaning. And the primal connection of love that is the foundation of creation is what nourishes us all at the deepest level—and, paradoxically, what we all search for, knowingly or unknowingly.

We are at the center of so many connections, and yet so easily we imagine ourselves isolated and alone.

ALCHEMY OF LIGHT: WORKING WITH THE PRIMAL ENERGIES OF LIFE

From the innermost plane, beyond even the primal emptiness, a light shines into the substance of life. Without this light nothing would exist: the atoms would not spin, the dawn would not come, the stars would not shine. And yet there are clouds that cover us, trying to obscure it. And the soul of creation is crying, needing the nourishment that comes from the Source, from that place which is no place.

And those of us who are the keepers of the light of the world know the danger and the dance at this time. Mostly we watch; we watch the patterns of forgetfulness that cover more and more of the Earth, we watch the light of those who aspire. We watch, always we watch.

INTO THE LIGHT AND BACK AGAIN: A MYSTIC'S JOURNEY

And then there are other stories that take us on their journey from beyond distant horizons. These are the stories I have been drawn to live, of visions of other worlds, unseen but potent beyond my imagination. Stories of light and darkness, of what is sacred and what is forgotten. These stories haunt me, often because they are mostly unsaid, or do not belong to the more recognized landscape of our lives. They do not fit into familiar patterns, but speak of a vaster landscape, of wisdom we have lost or a future we dare not see.

"Walking Between Worlds"

Those who have been drawn inward know the wonders of the inner world. We have seen its landscapes of light in our dreams and visions, heard its celestial music, carried its fragrance into our lives. We have learned to be nourished by the inner while we live in a world that seems to have forgotten its existence.

Spiritual Power: How It Works

Everything, every particle in creation, is surrounded by and infused with divine light. We do not see it because we are veiled by our own darkness and forgetfulness, but it is the light of the creation remembering its Creator, or the light of the Creator's own self-expression—the brush stroke of the Great Artist. This light carries the alchemy of creation: it is the *spirit mercurius* alive in this world. It is the miracle of rebirth that belongs to matter, in which matter celebrates the bond between the Creator and the creation.

FRAGMENTS OF A LOVE STORY: REFLECTIONS ON THE LIFE OF A MYSTIC

Just as human beings contain a sacred substance within our soul, there is a substance in the core of life that is real. It is like a seed of Truth, a spark of the light of the Absolute.

FOR LOVE OF THE REAL: A STORY OF LIFE'S MYSTICAL SECRET

There is a place, beyond the here and now. It is tended by angels, and the light is too bright for eyes to see. It welcomes strangers, and those who belong only to love. It is sad how we have forgotten this place, a place of perfection beyond even the shores of desolation. Yet those who travel there cannot forget, even if there is no mind, no images to remember. It remains a light in the darkness of the world, a place of refuge amidst the troubles of what we call life. It is as it always was—there are no seasons, no passing of the days. Remember this place, when it seems you are far away, when it seems that the river runs dry or the cry of the soul is too intense to bear.

INTO THE LIGHT AND BACK AGAIN:<br>A MYSTIC'S JOURNEY

Once there was a journey, like a story, an inner journey that echoed an outer journey, what we might call life. And then the unknown came calling, came crying in the night, in the depths of the heart, in the secret places of the soul. And the unknown took me away, without asking—only I blindly gave myself because I knew no other way to be.

INTO THE LIGHT AND BACK AGAIN:<br>A MYSTIC'S JOURNEY

The Truth is wild and raw, primal, as well as featureless and desolate beyond belief. It confuses, bewilders, intoxicates us; it makes us crazy; it leaves us lost. It shatters every concept, every image, every semblance of self. And yet it is the root of the root of all that exists and does not exist. It is present in every atom and every heartbeat, and with it comes love's ocean, limitless and dangerous. The desire for Truth is a drug, a poison that demands all of us again and again.

INTO THE LIGHT AND BACK AGAIN:<br>A MYSTIC'S JOURNEY

What are we made of, what is this combination of light and dust? So fragile, so tender, so deeply vulnerable, and yet so infinite, endless, vast beyond imagining. How can these two come together, how can the worlds meet to be woven into the single thread of love that is all that really exists? What is this mystery that I live, this constant undoing, this moment-by-moment wonder that contains all that is? Breath by breath we die and are reborn; breath by breath this mystery comes into form. And we are this mystery, this deepening silence, this uncovering we can never fully understand. We are the thread and our life the needle that sews the pattern....

INTO THE LIGHT AND BACK AGAIN:<br>A MYSTIC'S JOURNEY

In the end prayer and a place of prayer are all I have to offer, all I have to live....

My real companions are silence and prayer: the silence that knows me, that asks nothing and is always present. And prayer, that place where the worlds come together, where unknowing is an answer, where tears sometimes fall. Prayer is the friend of these my later years, when activity is for others, those who are still turning the pages of life. I prefer prayer, where the heart turns on its own, where the silence is part of me. Sometimes love is also present; sometimes the heart aches. Prayer knows these siblings, love and heartache, and prayer does not expect any answer.

INTO THE LIGHT AND BACK AGAIN:
A MYSTIC'S JOURNEY

I used to look for answers, but that was long ago. More and more as I get older I prefer to remain in unknowing, like when I first sat in meditation half a century ago, not expecting anything, but being taken into wonder. This for me is prayer, is spirit, is love, is watching a spring bud open on the plum tree in my garden.

"IN CONVERSATION—BJÖRK & LLEWELLYN VAUGHAN-LEE"

The eternal Essence is unchanging, "He is as He was."[6] There is no evolution, because It is complete unto Itself.[7] Yet from this unchangeable Essence pours out a constantly changing world, beautiful in its fragility. And our human experience is to be a vulnerable, transient partner of its moment-by-moment revelation. We are both witness and participant. We live its changing seasons, and within its cycles are also the seasons of our soul. As I feel the autumn of my own life, I sense a deep change, as if this unchanging Essence and my own story have become woven together in a new way, even though they were never separate.

Into the Light and Back Again:
A Mystic's Journey

I know the worlds of light and have experienced a darkness without light or love, just as every day I see an Earth that is forgetting Its song. It is my prayer that the worlds come more closely together, that the rivers of light can flow into the polluted waters of this world, and the light of divine purpose shine in even the darkest, most forgotten corners of our world.

Into the Light and Back Again:
A Mystic's Journey

Beyond the horizons of this world is a place that few know, a place without borders, without loss or gain, where even the cry of the seagull is forgotten. When you come here, or are taken here, remember this: here are no memories, not even silence, for silence would suggest the existence of sound. And yet something within you mysteriously recognizes what you have lost, recognizes the primal emptiness, the vast unknowing, the wonder of what is not. What is there to say of this place beyond the worlds? Here there are no dreams, there is no substance to form even images. And yet there is a belonging that is stamped in the core of one's being, a belonging that nothing can break.

FRAGMENTS OF A LOVE STORY: REFLECTIONS
ON THE LIFE OF A MYSTIC

And so the journey continues.... Your heart takes you to places that do not exist, where the snow falls gently and the wind comes from behind the clouds. And here, in this land, you can forget everything, even your own existence. There is no mirror to reflect you, no open door to walk through, just an endless landscape of love that knows no boundaries. And the wind is real and the snow continues to fall and the love continues, and will always continue. So you can leave behind those old worn clothes that you called your existence, those ways you used to walk when you thought you were alive. Because here in this place that is like no other there is the freedom you always knew, a freedom that belongs to love.

FRAGMENTS OF A LOVE STORY: REFLECTIONS
ON THE LIFE OF A MYSTIC

Do not be discouraged, do not ever be discouraged, even when you feel so lost and misunderstood, when the wheels of existence carry you always along roads you would rather not travel. There is this other land, this landscape that belongs to love. This is the place where the two seas meet, where existence reveals its secrets, where time uncovers what always was, even if you have never seen it before.

Fragments of a Love Story: Reflections on the Life of a Mystic

This world is not as we think; it is made from a substance that is not of atoms or particles, and in its depths there is a hidden song. Maybe at some moments in my life I have touched this substance, caught a line of this song. Maybe I have felt the heart of the world in my dreams, or while walking one still early morning. And so these pages leave traces, footprints that come to the water's edge. The sand is always shifting, the shoreline moves, and the currents of love's ocean run deeper than we can ever know.

Into the Light and Back Again: A Mystic's Journey

# EPILOGUE

So many thousands of years ago we were awakened to the wonder and magic of divine presence in the world around us. And the same light that awoke the Earth is what calls us back to love within the heart, so that the world should not forget. In my own life, since I was sixteen I have tried to live this light, both in its moment-by-moment revelation in the outer world—the light shining, reflected on the waters of the world—and in the deepening mystery of the inner worlds. I have tried to share some of its secrets, even though words cannot capture its brightness. It is like a koan that breaks the patterns of the mind, too clear and simple to be understood, only grasped. I hope that it has found its way through the spaces between my words, places that have been left empty. I do know that it is present in the heartbeat of the world, and this morning it greeted me in the sunlight after the fog.

# NOTES

1. *Hadith qudsi*. See also ‘Abd al-Qadir al-Jilani, *The Secret of Secrets (Sirr al-Asrar)*, p. 15. Further he notes:

   The vision of Allah is of two kinds: one is seeing the manifestation of Allah’s attribute of Perfect Beauty directly in the hereafter, and the other is seeing the manifestation of the divine attributes reflected upon the clear mirror of the pure heart, in this life, in this world. In such a case the vision appears as the manifestation of light emanating from the Perfect Beauty of Allah and is seen by the eye of the essence of the heart. (Ibid., p. 51.)

   The purpose of the creation of this universe is to discover, to see that hidden treasure. Allah says through His Prophet, “I was a hidden treasure, I willed to be known. I created the creation so that I would be known.” That is to say, that He would be known in this material world through His attributes manifested in His creation. But to see His very Essence is left to the hereafter. There, the vision of Allah will be direct, as He wills, and it will be the eye of the child of the heart that sees Him. (Ibid., p. 53.)

2. The poet William Wordsworth describes this sad transition:

   Heaven lies about us in our infancy!
   Shades of the prison-house begin to close
   Upon the growing Boy
   But He beholds the light and whence it flows.
   He sees it in his joy; …
   At length the Man perceives it die away,
   And fade into the light of common day.

   “Intimations of Immortality from Recollections of Early Childhood,” ll. 66–76, *Wordsworth Poetical Works*.

3. The light hidden within the created world is what the alchemists called the *lumen naturae.*

4. The "naming" of creation was an important step in the spiritual evolution of the Earth. In the Bible, in Genesis, Adam named "every living creature," (2:19). In the Qur'an (2:31) it is written that "He taught Adam the names, all of them," meaning that Adam was taught the inner nature and qualities of all things. And so the first man had knowledge of the names of creation, which belong to the divine "secrets of heaven and earth," Qur'an (2:33).

5. The "magic" referred to here is life's natural magic, for example when synchronicities happen, or one is guided by dreams or visions, or the "earth magic" when a plant communicates to a shaman or healer its healing properties. Magic that is used for personal power or gain is different, as it is directed by the ego, and does not belong to the natural flow of life from the inner to the outer world. It was the earliest misuse of magic, many thousands of years ago, that began the split between the worlds, sometimes described as the Fall.

6. *Hadith.*

7. "When He called into being the things that are, He was already endowed with all His attributes, and He is as He was then. In His oneness there is no difference between what is recent and what is original." Ibn 'Arabi, *Al-Futuhat al-Makkiyya: The Meccan Revelations.*

# BIBLIOGRAPHY

## BOOKS

*Alchemy of Light: Working with the Primal Energies of Life*, The Golden Sufi Center, 2007, and second edition 2019.

*Awakening the World: A Global Dimension to Spiritual Practice*, The Golden Sufi Center, 2006 (updated edition is *Including the Earth in Our Prayers*, 2019).

*Catching the Thread: Sufism, Dreamwork, and Jungian Psychology*, The Golden Sufi Center, 1998.

*Darkening of the Light: Witnessing the End of an Era*, The Golden Sufi Center, 2013.

*For Love of the Real: A Story of Life's Mystical Secret*, Llewellyn Vaughan-Lee with Hilary Hart, The Golden Sufi Center, 2015.

*Fragments of a Love Story: Reflections on the Life of a Mystic*, The Golden Sufi Center, 2011.

*In the Company of Friends: Dreamwork Within a Sufi Group*, The Golden Sufi Center, 1994.

*Including the Earth in Our Prayers: A Global Dimension to Spiritual Practice* (updated edition of *Awakening the Earth*), The Golden Sufi Center, 2019.

*Into the Light and Back Again: A Mystic's Journey*, Unpublished: The Golden Sufi Center, 2020.

*Light of Oneness*, The Golden Sufi Center, 2004.

*Love is a Fire: The Sufi's Mystical Journey Home*, The Golden Sufi Center, 2000.

*Prayer of the Heart in Christian and Sufi Mysticism*, The Golden Sufi Center, 2012.

*Sacred Seed: A Collection of Essays*, edited by The Global Peace Initiative of Women, The Golden Sufi Center, 2014.

*Seasons of the Sacred: Reconnecting to the Wisdom Within Nature and the Soul*, The Golden Sufi Center, 2021.

*Spiritual Ecology: 10 Practices to Reawaken the Sacred in Everyday Life*, Llewellyn Vaughan-Lee with Hilary Hart, The Golden Sufi Center, 2017.

*Spiritual Ecology: The Cry of the Earth*, edited by Llewellyn Vaughan-Lee, The Golden Sufi Center, 2013, and second edition 2016.

*Spiritual Power: How It Works*, The Golden Sufi Center, 2005, and second edition 2019.

*Sufism: The Transformation of the Heart*, The Golden Sufi Center, 1995.

*The Bond with the Beloved: The Mystical Relationship of Lover and Beloved*, The Golden Sufi Center, 1993.

*The Circle of Love*, The Golden Sufi Center, 1999.

*The Face Before I Was Born: A Spiritual Autobiography*, The Golden Sufi Center, 1997, and second edition 2009.

*The Paradoxes of Love*, The Golden Sufi Center, 1996.

*The Return of the Feminine and World Soul*, The Golden Sufi Center, 2009, and second edition 2017.

*The Signs of God*, The Golden Sufi Center, 2001.

*Travelling the Path of Love: Sayings of Sufi Masters*, Llewellyn Vaughan-Lee, editor, The Golden Sufi Center, 1995.

*Working with Oneness*, The Golden Sufi Center, 2002.

## ARTICLES, AUDIO, and VIDEO

"7 Days of Rest: A Time to Heal" video, from *7 Days of Rest*, recorded in Point Reyes Station, California, January 2018.

"A Dream of the Earth," audio with transcript, from *Stories for a Living Future Podcast, Series 2: From the Edge of the World*, recorded in Inverness, California, June 15, 2023.

"A Four-Point Plan Revisited," audio with transcript, from *Stories for a Living Future Podcast, Series 2: From the Edge of the World*, recorded in Inverness, California, April 6, 2023.

"A Hidden Pathway," audio with transcript, from *Stories for a Living Future Podcast, Series 1*, recorded in Inverness, California, June 1, 2022.

"A New Note in the Axis of Love," audio with transcript, from *Stories for a Living Future Podcast, Series 2: From the Edge of the World*, recorded in Inverness, California, May 18, 2023.

"A Return to Love," audio with transcript, from *Stories for a Living Future Podcast, Series 4: My Own Story*, recorded in Inverness, California, June 6, 2024.

"A Return to Love: A Few Simple Words for Mystics and Lovers," video with transcript, The Golden Sufi Center, March 2020.

"A Story of Beginnings: A Personal Story of Memories of Magic and Wonder," audio with transcript, from *Stories for a Living Future Podcast, Series 1*, recorded in Inverness, California, December 1, 2022.

"A Time for Silence," article, *The Garrison Institute*, November 2017.

"Angels and Devas," audio with transcript, from *Stories for a Living Future Podcast, Series 3: Stories of the Heart*, recorded in Inverness, California, November 16, 2023.

"Changing the Story," article, *The Garrison Institute*, August 2018.

"Earth Changes," audio with transcript, from *Stories for a Living Future Podcast, Series 2: From the Edge of the World*, recorded in Inverness, California, June 29, 2023.

"Fire Season," article, *Parabola*, Autumn 2021.

"Global Citizens of a Living Earth," article, interview with Rhonda Fabian for *Kosmos Journal*, February 19, 2015.

"In Conversation—Björk and Llewellyn Vaughan-Lee," article, Björk's Cornucopia Tour Book, July 2019.

"Including the Earth in Our Prayers: Spiritual Practice as a Catalyst for Change," article, *Kosmos Journal*, September 2019.

"Into the Light and Back Again," audio with transcript, from *Stories for a Living Future Podcast, Series 3: Stories of the Heart*, recorded in Inverness, California, December 14, 2023.

"Introduction: Stories for a Living Future," audio with transcript, from *Stories for a Living Future Podcast, Series 1*, recorded in Inverness, California, October 19, 2022.

"Introduction: Stories of the Heart," audio with transcript, from *Stories for a Living Future Podcast, Series 3: Stories of the Heart*, recorded in Inverness, California, September 14, 2023.

"Invoking the World Soul," audio with transcript, recorded at the event *Working with the Sacred Substance of Life*, Seattle, Washington, May 18, 2007.

"Listening to the Wind," audio with transcript, from S*tories for a Living Future Podcast, Series 3: Stories of the Heart*, recorded in Inverness, California, September 21, 2023.

"Living Oneness," audio with transcript, from *Stories for a Living Future Podcast, Series 2: From the Edge of the World*, recorded in Inverness, California, July 13, 2023.

"Living the Moment of the Soul," article, *Caduceus Journal*, 1999.

"Loneliness and the Sacred Web of Life," article, *Huffington Post*, March 2014.

"Love and Prayer," audio with transcript, from S*tories for a Living Future Podcast, Series 3: Stories of the Heart*, recorded in Inverness, California, October 19, 2023.

"Love: Life's Greatest Gift," article, *Common Ground*, February 2017.

"Lover and Beloved: Mystical Love in Sufism," article, The Golden Sufi Center, August 3, 2023.

"Meaning and the Song of the Soul," article, *Excellence Reporter*, February 2016.

"Sacred Time," article, *Parabola*, May 2023.

"Seasons of the Sacred: Sacred Time," article, *Heartfulness*, August 2021.

"Seeding the Future," article, *The Great Turning: Living Earth*, November 3, 2021.

"Spiritual Ecology," article, *Seven Pillars House of Wisdom*, August 2009.

"Sustainability, Deep Ecology, and the Sacred," article, *Huffington Post*, April 2013.

"The Call of the Earth," article, *Parabola*, Autumn 2013.

"The Gift of a Garden," audio with transcript, from *Stories for a Living Future Podcast, Series 2: From the Edge of the World*, recorded in Inverness, California, May 4, 2023.

"The Living Moment: Reflections of an Old Man," audio with transcript, from *Stories for a Living Future Podcast, Series 2: From the Edge of the World*, recorded in Inverness, California, July 27, 2023.

"The Magic of Creation," article, *Sutra Journal*, Spring 2016.

"The Natural Order of Things," article, *Parabola*, Autumn 2020.

"The One Quality Needed for the Path," video, recorded at the event series *Where the Two Seas Meet,* Bay Conference Center, Tiburon, California, November 2009.

"The Space Between Stories," audio with transcript, from *Stories for a Living Future Podcast*: *Interlude between Series 1 and 2*, recorded in Inverness, California, March 9, 2023.

"Threads of Love," audio with transcript, from *Stories for a Living Future Podcast, Series 1*, recorded in Inverness, California, November 17, 2022.

"Unity and the Power of Love," article, *Kosmos Journal*, Autumn 2018.

"Walking Between Worlds," audio with transcript, from *Stories for a Living Future Podcast, Series 4: My Own Story*, recorded in Inverness, California, June 27, 2024.

"Watching at the Edge of the World," audio with transcript, from *Stories for a Living Future Podcast, Series 2: From the Edge of the World*, recorded in Inverness, California, March 23, 2023.

"Watching the Stars," audio with transcript, from *Stories for a Living Future Podcast, Series 2: From the Edge of the World*, recorded in Inverness, California, August 10, 2023.

"We Are All One: Interview with Llewellyn Vaughan-Lee," video, *One: The Movie*, Circle of Bliss Productions, recorded in Inverness, California, Autumn 2002.

"When the Source Ran Free," audio with transcript, from *Stories for a Living Future Podcast, Series 1*, recorded in Inverness, California, October 27, 2022.

"Where the Horses Sing," article with audio, *Emergence Magazine*, May 2021.

"Words," audio with transcript, from *Stories for a Living Future Podcast, Series 1*, recorded in Inverness, California, January 12, 2023.

Additional resources from Llewellyn Vaughan-Lee, including further articles, books, and audio and video recordings, can be found at goldensufi.org and workingwithoneness.org.

## ABOUT THE AUTHOR

LLEWELLYN VAUGHAN-LEE, Ph.D., is a Sufi teacher and author. Born in London in 1953, he has followed the Naqshbandi Sufi path since he was nineteen. In 1991 he moved with his family to Northern California and founded The Golden Sufi Center (www.goldensufi.org). He has written a series of books giving a detailed exploration of the stages of spiritual and psychological transformation experienced on the Sufi path, with a particular focus on the use of dreamwork as inner guidance on the journey. Since 2000 the focus of his writing and teaching has been an emerging global consciousness of oneness, spiritual ecology, and the need for a spiritual response to our present ecological crisis (see *Spiritual Ecology: The Cry of the Earth*). He has also been featured in the TV series Global Spirit and was interviewed by Oprah Winfrey as a part of her Super Soul Sunday series.

## ABOUT THE PUBLISHER

The Golden Sufi Center publishes books, video, and audio on Sufism and mysticism. A California religious nonprofit 501(c)(3) corporation, it is dedicated to making the teachings of the Naqshbandi Sufi path available to all seekers.

THE GOLDEN SUFI CENTER
P.O. Box 456 · Point Reyes Station · CA · 94956-0456
www.goldensufi.org